GRADES
K-2

the Super Source®
Base Ten Blocks

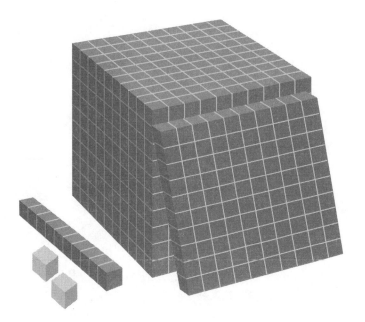

ETA/Cuisenaire®
Vernon Hills, Illinois 60061-1862

800-445-5985

www.etacuisenaire.com

Dedication

To Jeffrey B. Sellon, whose leadership, creativity,
and passion for manipulatives inspired *the Super Source*®

To the many teachers and students across the country
who ensured the success of *the Super Source*® by participating
in the outlining, writing, and field testing of the materials

Executive Editor: Doris Hirschhorn
Editorial Manager: John Nelson
Project Editor: Harriet Slonim
Lessons Creators/Writers: Amy Feldman, Jane Crawford
Field Test Coordinator: Laurie Verdeschi

Design Director: Jim O'Shea
Production/Manufacturing Coordinator: Roxanne Knoll
Cover Design: Phyllis Aycock
Illustrations: Rebecca Thornburgh

ETA/Cuisenaire
500 Greenview Court • Vernon Hills, Illinois 60061-1862
www.etacuisenaire.com • 800-445-5985

Table of Contents

Using the Super Source®

The Super Source is a series of books, each of which contains a collection of activities to use with a specific math manipulative. Driving **the Super Source** is ETA/Cuisenaire's conviction that children construct their own understandings through rich, hands-on mathematical experiences. Although the activities in each book are written for a specific grade range, they all connect to the core of mathematics learning that is important to every K–6 child. Thus, the material in many activities can easily be refocused for children at other grade levels. Because the activities are not arranged sequentially, children can work on any activity at any time.

The lessons in **the Super Source** all follow a basic structure consistent with the vision of mathematics teaching described in the *Curriculum and Evaluation Standards for School Mathematics* published by the National Council of Teachers of Mathematics. All of the activities in this series involve Problem Solving, Communication, Reasoning, and Mathematical Connections—the first four NCTM Standards. Each activity also focuses on one or more of the following curriculum strands: Number, Geometry, Measurement, Patterns/Functions, Probability/Statistics, and Logic.

HOW LESSONS ARE ORGANIZED

At the beginning of each lesson you will find, to the right of the title, both the major curriculum strands to which the lesson relates and the particular topics that children will work with. Each lesson has three main sections. The first, GETTING READY, offers an *Overview,* which states what children will be doing and why, and provides a list of "What You'll Need." Specific numbers of Base Ten Blocks are suggested on this list but can be adjusted as the needs of your specific situation dictate. Before an activity, blocks can be counted out and placed in containers or self-sealing plastic bags for easy distribution. When crayons are called for, it is understood that markers may be used instead. Blackline masters that are provided for your convenience at the back of the book are also referenced on this materials list. Paper, pencils, scissors, tape, and materials for making charts, which may be necessary in certain activities, are usually not.

Although overhead Base Ten Blocks and the suggestion to make overhead transparencies of the blackline masters are always listed in "What You'll Need" as optional, these materials are highly effective when you want to demonstrate the use of Base Ten Blocks. As you move blocks on the screen, children can work with the same materials at their seats. If overhead Base Ten Blocks are not available, you may want to make and use transparencies of the Base Ten Block shapes and a place-value mat. Children can also use the overhead Base Ten Blocks and/or a transparency of the place-value mat to present their work to other members of their group or to the class.

The second section, THE ACTIVITY, first presents a possible scenario for *Introducing* the children to the activity. The aim of this brief introduction is to help you give children the tools they will need to investigate independently. However, care has been taken to avoid undercutting the activity itself. Since these investigations are designed to enable children to increase their own mathematical power, the idea is to set the stage but not steal the show! The heart of the lesson, *On Their Own,* is found in a box at the top of the second page of each lesson. Here, rich problems stimulate many different problem-solving approaches and lead to a variety of solutions. These hands-on explorations have the potential for bringing children to new mathematical ideas and deepening skills.

On Their Own is intended as a stand-alone activity for children to explore with a partner or in a small group. Be sure to make the needed directions clearly visible. You may want to write them on the chalkboard or on an overhead or present them either on reusable cards or paper. For children who may have difficulty reading the directions, you can read them aloud or make sure that at least one "reader" is in each group.

The last part of this second section, *The Bigger Picture*, gives suggestions for how children can share their work and their thinking and make mathematical connections. Class charts and children's recorded work provide a springboard for discussion. Under "Thinking and Sharing" there are several prompts that you can use to promote discussion. Children will not be able to respond to these prompts with one-word answers. Instead, the prompts encourage children to describe what they notice, tell how they found their results, and give the reasoning behind their answers. Thus children learn to verify their own results rather than relying on the teacher to determine if an answer is "right" or "wrong." Though the class discussion might immediately follow the investigation, it is important not to cut the activity short by having a class discussion too soon.

The Bigger Picture often includes a suggestion for a "Writing" (or drawing) assignment. This is meant to help children process what they have just been doing. You might want to use these ideas as a focus for daily or weekly entries in a math journal that each child keeps.

<table>
<tr>
<td>

If it has 2 digits the number is between 10-99. If the number is 7 it is 1 digit if the number is 100 it is 3 digit.

</td>
<td>

You look at the blocks and you look at the paper and amagin how many there are.

</td>
</tr>
<tr>
<td align="center">From: **Number Builder**</td>
<td align="center">From: **How Many Can You Hold?**</td>
</tr>
</table>

The Bigger Picture always ends with ideas for "Extending the Activity." Extensions take the essence of the main activity and either alter or extend its parameters. These activities are well used with a class that becomes deeply involved in the primary activity or for children who finish before the others. In any case, it is probably a good idea to expose the entire class to the possibility of, and the results from, such extensions.

The third and final section of the lesson is TEACHER TALK. Here, in *Where's the Mathematics?*, you can gain insight into the underlying mathematics of the activity and discover some of the strategies children are apt to use as they work. Solutions are also given—when such are necessary and/or helpful. Because *Where's the Mathematics?* provides a view of what may happen in the lesson as well as the underlying mathematical potential that may grow out of it, this may be the section that you want to read before presenting the activity to children.

USING THE ACTIVITIES

The Super Source has been designed to fit into the variety of classroom environments in which it will be used. These range from a completely manipulative-based classroom to one in which manipulatives are just beginning to play a part. You may choose to use some activities in *the Super Source* in the way set forth in each lesson (introducing an activity to the whole class, then breaking up the class into groups that all work on the same task, and so forth). You will then be able to circulate among the groups as they work to observe and perhaps comment on each child's work. This approach requires a full classroom set of materials but allows you to concentrate on the variety of ways that children respond to a given activity.

Alternatively, you may wish to make two or three related activities available to different groups of children at the same time. You may even wish to use different manipulatives to explore the same mathematical concept. (Snap™ Cubes and Cuisenaire® Rods, for example, can be used to teach some of the same principles as Base Ten Blocks.) This approach does not require full classroom sets of a particular manipulative. It also permits greater adaptation of materials to individual children's needs and/or preferences.

If children are comfortable working independently, you might want to set up a "menu"—that is, set out a number of related activities from which children can choose. Children should be encouraged to write about their experiences with these independent activities.

However you choose to use *the Super Source* activities, it would be wise to allow time for several groups or the entire class to share their experiences. The dynamics of this type of interaction, where children share not only solutions and strategies but also feelings and intuitions, is the basis of continued mathematical growth. It allows children who are beginning to form a mathematical structure to clarify it and those who have mastered just isolated concepts to begin to see how these concepts might fit together.

Again, both the individual teaching style and combined learning styles of the children should dictate the specific method of utilizing *the Super Source* lessons. At first sight, some activities may appear too difficult for some of your children, and you may find yourself tempted to actually "teach" by modeling exactly how an activity can lead to a particular learning outcome. If you do this, you rob children of the chance to try the activity in whatever way they can. As long as children have a way to begin an investigation, give them time and opportunity to see it through. Instead of making assumptions about what children will or won't do, watch and listen. The excitement and challenge of the activity—as well as the chance to work cooperatively—may bring out abilities in children that will surprise you.

If you are convinced, however, that an activity does not suit your students, adjust it, by all means. You may want to change the language, either by simplifying it or by referring to specific vocabulary that you and your children already use and are comfortable with. On the other hand, if you suspect that an activity isn't challenging enough, you may want to read through the activity extensions for a variation that you can give children instead.

RECORDING

Although the direct process of working with Base Ten Blocks is a valuable one, it is afterward, when children look at, compare, share, and think about their constructions and arrangements, that an activity yields its greatest rewards. However, because Base Ten Block activity results can't always be left intact for very long, children need an effective way to record their work. To this end, at the back of this book recording paper is provided for reproduction. The "What You'll Need" listing at the beginning of each lesson often specifies the kind of recording paper to use. For example, in an activity where children are working only with units, longs, and flats, they can duplicate their work or trace the block pieces on the Base Ten Block Grid Paper (1-centimeter grid paper) found on page 109.

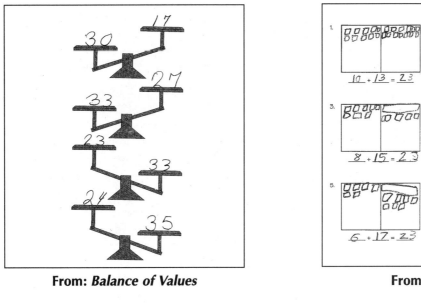

From: *Balance of Values*

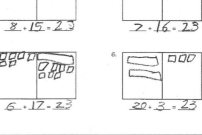

From: *Sum It Up*

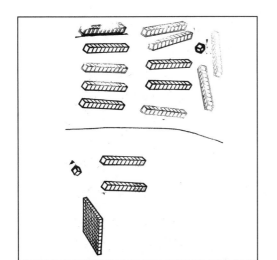

From: *Number Builder*

From: *Feed the Birds*

You may want to have some children record their work on 2-centimeter grid paper to provide them with larger areas to color. Other children may be able to use grids with squares that are even smaller than 1 square centimeter. These children may also be able to use the blocks as templates to trace their results on unlined paper.

When young children initially explore with Base Ten Blocks, they are likely to use up every available block in making a huge pattern. A pattern of this size can be daunting for a child to record. Such patterns may be recorded using cutouts of the Base Ten Block shapes. (You may wish to reproduce the outlines of flats, longs, and units found on pages 110–112 and then cut the shapes apart.) Children can color the shapes and paste them in place on unlined paper.

Another interesting way to "freeze" a Base Ten Block design or construction is to create it using the appropriate software and then print it. Children can use a classroom or resource-room computer if it is available or, where possible, extend the activity into a home assignment by utilizing their home computers.

Recording involves more than copying the designs. Writing, drawing, and making charts and tables are also ways to record. By creating a table of data gathered in the course of their investigations, children are able to draw conclusions and look for patterns. When children write or draw, either in their group or later by themselves, they are clarifying their understanding of their recent mathematical experience.

From: *Build a Bug House*

From: *What Price Lunch?*

From: *Way to Pay*

From: *Number Builder*

With a roomful of children busily engaged in their investigations, it is not easy for a teacher to keep track of how individual children are working. Having tangible material to gather and examine when the time is right will help you to keep in close touch with each child's learning.

Exploring Base Ten Blocks

The Base Ten Blocks provide a spatial model of our base ten number system. The smallest blocks, cubes that measure 1 cm on a side, represent ones. These are called *units.* The long, narrow blocks that measure 10 cm by 1 cm by 1 cm represent tens. These are called *longs.* The flat, square blocks that measure 10 cm by 10 cm by 1 cm represent hundreds. These are called *flats.* The largest blocks available, cubes that measure 10 cm on a side, represent thousands. These are called *cubes.*

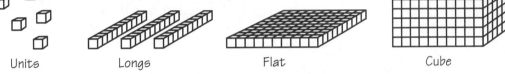

Units   Longs   Flat   Cube

The size relationships among the blocks make them ideal for the investigation of number concepts. Initially, however, children should explore independently with Base Ten Blocks before engaging in structured activities. As they move the blocks around to create designs and build structures, they may be able to discover on their own that it takes ten of a smaller block to make one of the next larger block. Children's designs and structures also lead them to employ spatial visualization and to work intuitively with the geometric concepts of shape, perimeter, area, and volume.

Base Ten Blocks are especially useful in providing children with ways to physically represent the concepts of place value and addition, subtraction, multiplication, and division of whole numbers. By building number combinations with Base Ten Blocks, children ease into the concept of regrouping, or trading, and are able to see the logical development of each operation. The blocks provide a visual foundation and understanding of the algorithms children use when doing paper-and-pencil computation. Older children can transfer their understanding of whole numbers and whole-number operations to an understanding of decimals and decimal operations.

WORKING WITH BASE TEN BLOCKS

Place-value mats, available in pads of 50, provide a means for children to organize their work as they explore the relationships among the blocks and determine how groups of blocks can be used to represent numbers. Children may begin by placing unit blocks, one at a time, in the units column on a mat. For each unit they place, they record the number corresponding to the total number of units placed (1, 2, 3, ...). They continue this process until they have accumulated 10 units, at which point they match their 10 units to 1 long and trade those units for the long, which they place in the longs column. They continue in the same way, adding units one at a time to the units column and recording the totals (11, 12, 13, ...) until it is time to trade for a second long, which they place in the longs column (20). When they finally come to 99, there are 9 units and 9 longs on the mat. Adding one more unit forces two trades: first 10 units for another long and then 10 longs for a flat (100). Then it is time to continue adding and recording units and making trades as needed as children work their way through the hundreds and up to thousands. Combining the placing and trading of longs with the act of recording the corresponding numbers provides children with a connection between concrete and symbolic representations of numbers.

Base Ten Blocks can be used to develop understanding of the meanings of addition, subtraction, multiplication, and division. Modeling addition on a place-value mat provides children with a visual basis for the concept of regrouping.

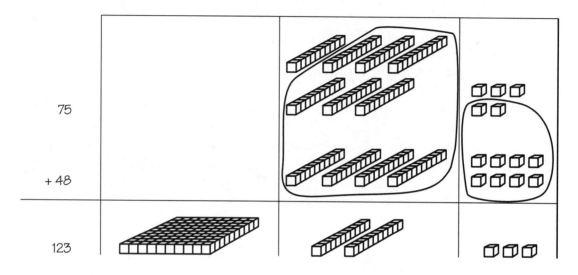

Subtraction with regrouping involves trading some of the blocks used to model the minuend of a subtraction example for smaller blocks of equal value so that the "taking away" can be accomplished. For example, in order to subtract 15 from 32, a child would trade one of the longs that represent 32 (3 longs and 2 units) for 10 units to form an equivalent representation of 32 (2 longs and 12 units). Then the child would take away 15 (1 long and 5 units) and be left with a difference of 17 (1 long and 7 units).

Multiplication can be modeled as repeated addition or with rectangular arrays. Using rectangular arrays can help in understanding the derivation of the partial products, the sum of which is the total product.

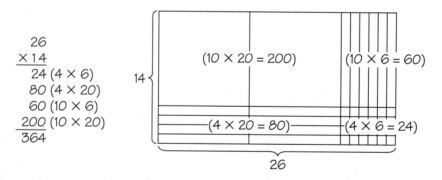

Division can be done as repeated subtraction or through building and analyzing structures and rectangular arrays.

By letting the cube, flat, long, and unit represent 1, 0.1, 0.01, and 0.001, respectively, older children can explore and develop decimal concepts, compare decimals, and perform basic operations with decimal numbers.

The squares along each face make the blocks excellent tools for visualizing and internalizing the concepts of perimeter and surface area of structures. Counting unit blocks in a structure can form the basis for understanding and finding volume.

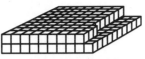

perimeter of base = 24 cm
surface area = 112 cm²
volume = 60 cm³

perimeter of base = 40 cm
surface area = 278 cm²
volume = 183 cm³

ASSESSING CHILDREN'S UNDERSTANDING

The use of Base Ten Blocks provides a perfect opportunity for authentic assessment. Watching children work with the blocks gives you a sense of how they approach a mathematical problem. Their thinking can be "seen" through their positioning of the blocks. When a class breaks up into small working groups, you are able to circulate, listen, and raise questions, all the while focusing on how individuals are thinking.

The challenges that children encounter when working with Base Ten Blocks often elicit unexpected abilities from those whose performance in more symbolic, number-oriented tasks may be weak. On the other hand, some children with good memories for numerical relationships have difficulty with spatial challenges and can more readily learn from freely exploring with Base Ten Blocks. Thus, by observing children's free exploration, you can get a sense of individual styles and intellectual strengths.

Having children describe their creations and share their strategies and thinking with the whole class gives you another opportunity for observational assessment. Furthermore, you may want to gather children's recorded work or invite them to choose pieces to add to their math portfolios.

I would by ships for $1.5A I would use
1 flat 5 longs 9 units that would be the
lest number to by the ships

From: *Way to Pay*

I did 10 + 10 = 20 and
20 + 3 = 23 so I did
10 + 13 = 23. nekst I fond the
frst nudr and hind the
sekint.

From: *Sum It Up!*

Models of teachers assessing children's understanding can be found in Cuisenaire's series of videotapes listed below.

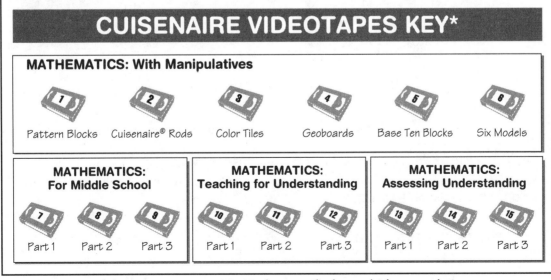

CUISENAIRE VIDEOTAPES KEY*

MATHEMATICS: With Manipulatives

| Pattern Blocks | Cuisenaire® Rods | Color Tiles | Geoboards | Base Ten Blocks | Six Models |

MATHEMATICS: For Middle School

| Part 1 | Part 2 | Part 3 |

MATHEMATICS: Teaching for Understanding

| Part 1 | Part 2 | Part 3 |

MATHEMATICS: Assessing Understanding

| Part 1 | Part 2 | Part 3 |

*See *Overview of the Lessons*, pages 16–17, for specific lesson/video correlation.

Connect *the Super Source®* **to NCTM Standards.**

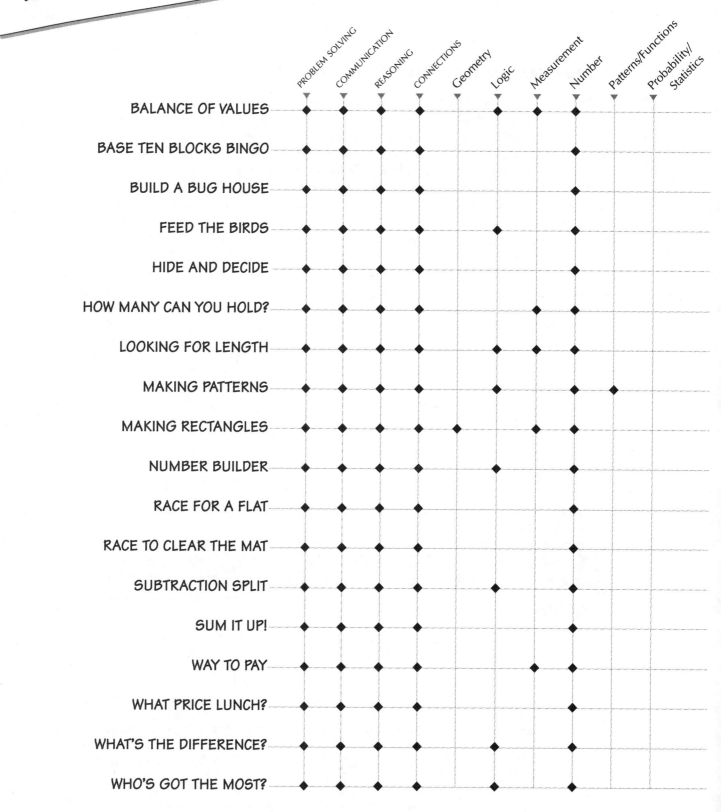

	PROBLEM SOLVING	COMMUNICATION	REASONING	CONNECTIONS	Geometry	Logic	Measurement	Number	Patterns/Functions	Probability/Statistics
BALANCE OF VALUES	◆	◆	◆	◆	◆	◆		◆		
BASE TEN BLOCKS BINGO	◆	◆	◆	◆				◆		
BUILD A BUG HOUSE	◆	◆	◆	◆						
FEED THE BIRDS	◆	◆	◆			◆		◆		
HIDE AND DECIDE	◆	◆	◆					◆		
HOW MANY CAN YOU HOLD?	◆	◆		◆			◆	◆		
LOOKING FOR LENGTH	◆	◆	◆			◆	◆			
MAKING PATTERNS	◆	◆	◆	◆				◆	◆	
MAKING RECTANGLES	◆	◆			◆		◆	◆		
NUMBER BUILDER	◆	◆				◆		◆		
RACE FOR A FLAT	◆	◆		◆				◆		
RACE TO CLEAR THE MAT	◆	◆		◆				◆		
SUBTRACTION SPLIT	◆	◆	◆			◆		◆		
SUM IT UP!	◆	◆	◆	◆				◆		
WAY TO PAY	◆	◆	◆				◆	◆		
WHAT PRICE LUNCH?	◆	◆	◆					◆		
WHAT'S THE DIFFERENCE?	◆	◆	◆					◆		
WHO'S GOT THE MOST?	◆	◆	◆	◆		◆		◆		

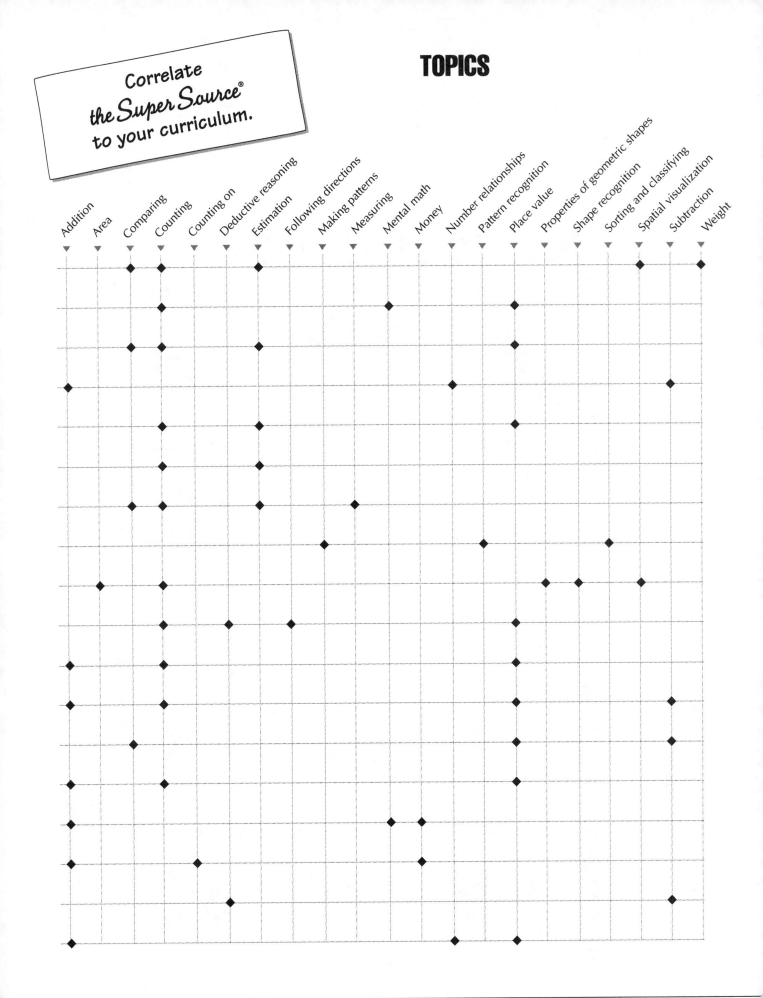

Correlate
the Super Source®
to your curriculum.

Addition · Area · Comparing · Counting · Counting on · Deductive reasoning · Estimation · Following directions · Making patterns · Measuring · Mental math · Money · Number relationships · Pattern recognition · Place value · Properties of geometric shapes · Shape recognition · Sorting and classifying · Spatial visualization · Subtraction · Weight

Classroom-tested activities contained in these *Super Source* Base Ten books focus on the math strands in the charts below.

...the Super Source® Base Ten, Grades 3–4

Geometry	Logic	Measurement
Number	Patterns/Functions	Probability/Statistics

...the Super Source® Base Ten, Grades 5–6

Geometry	Logic	Measurement
Number	Patterns/Functions	Probability/Statistics

Classroom-tested activities contained in these *Super Source* books focus on the math strands as indicated in these charts.

...the Super Source® Snap™ Cubes, Grades K–2

Geometry	Logic	Measurement
Number	Patterns/Functions	Probability/Statistics

...the Super Source® Tangrams, Grades K–2

Geometry	Logic	Measurement
Number	Patterns/Functions	Probability/Statistics

...the Super Source® Cuisenaire® Rods, Grades K–2

Geometry	Logic	Measurement
Number	Patterns/Functions	Probability/Statistics

...the Super Source® Geoboards, Grades K–2

Geometry	Logic	Measurement
Number	Patterns/Functions	Probability/Statistics

...the Super Source® Color Tiles, Grades K–2

Geometry	Logic	Measurement
Number	Patterns/Functions	Probability/Statistics

...the Super Source® Pattern Blocks, Grades K–2

Geometry	Logic	Measurement
Number	Patterns/Functions	Probability/Statistics

Overview of the Lessons

See video key, page 11.

Base Ten Blocks, Grades K–2

See video key, page 11.

BALANCE OF VALUES

- Spatial visualization
- Counting
- Comparing
- Estimation
- Weight

Getting Ready

What You'll Need

Base Ten Blocks, 1 set per pair

Small classroom objects

Balance scales

Small, self-sealing plastic lunch bags, 1 per child

Markers

Weighing Numbers worksheet, 1 per pair, page 90

The Activity

Overview

Children compare the values of different groups of Base Ten units. They do this by estimating, by weighing two groups of units and determining the heavier of the two, and then by counting to find how many more units are in the heavier group than in the lighter one. In this activity, children have the opportunity to:

- ◆ use spatial visualization to estimate
- ◆ count units and name the number they represent
- ◆ compare weights

Introducing

- ◆ Display a balance scale. Invite several volunteers to each choose two small objects, such as a pencil eraser and a glue stick, to weigh on the scale.

- ◆ Have the volunteers first hold one object in each hand and guess, or *estimate,* which of their two objects weighs more. Call them up, in turn, to place one of their objects in each pan of the scale.

- ◆ Ask children what they notice.

- ◆ If one pan appears to be lower than the other, ask which of the two objects weighs more. Elicit that the object in the lower pan is the heavier object, the one that weighs more, and that the object in the higher pan is the lighter object, the one that weighs less.

- ◆ Add units to the higher pan or take units off the lower pan—one at a time—until the scale balances. Point out that when the pans are the same height, (or when they form a straight line), they are "in balance." This means that the object in one pan weighs the same as the object in the other pan.

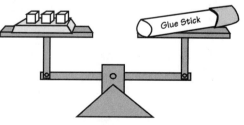

On Their Own

How can you use a balance scale to find which group of Base 10 Blocks has more?

- Work with a partner. Each of you write your name on a plastic bag. Grab a handful of units. Put them into the bag and close it.

- Estimate. Whose bag do you think has more units?

- Put 1 bag in each pan of a balance scale.

- Decide whose bag has more.

- Together count the units from each bag. Find 2 ways to figure out how many more units were in the heavier bag than in the lighter bag.

- Record the units in each bag on a worksheet that has balance scales.

- Do the activity 3 more times.

- The last time, put your units back into the bags. Leave the bags and your worksheet out where everyone can see them.

The Bigger Picture

Thinking and Sharing

Allow children to walk around the classroom to observe other children's work. Encourage them to stop and compare several pairs of bags, first estimating which of the two weighs more and then checking their estimates against the recordings.

Use prompts like these to promote class discussion:

- How did you make your estimates?

- How does a balance scale tell you if two things weigh exactly the same?

- How could you be sure of which bag had more units? How could you be sure of which bag had fewer units?

- If you had two bags of units that did not weigh the same, what would be a good way to make them weigh the same?

- Is it always possible to balance a balance scale? Explain.

Extending the Activity

1. Have pairs repeat the activity, but this time have them estimate which bag has less. Have them use the scale to check their estimates and then count to find how many fewer units the lighter bag has than the heavier one.

Teacher Talk

Where's the Mathematics?

In doing this balance-scale activity, one second grader came to realize that not only does the number of units in each pan determine balance, but the way in which the units are arranged on the two pans also affects balance. This understanding resulted from the teacher telling the girl to think about how to balance a see-saw. "What would you do if you were sitting on one side and a smaller person got on the other side?" (The child would move forward on her side, toward the middle.) "What if a larger person got on the other side?" (The child would move back on her side, toward the end.) Immediately, the girl caught on to the importance of balancing the scale by placing units on the two sides in about the same location on each pan.

In addition to using the balance scale to compare relative weights, children can use it to compare specific weights. Point out that each Base Ten unit block weighs one gram (1 g) and so, for example, a group of ten units weighs ten grams. Invite children to explore the equivalent weights of groups of units by placing one unit in each pan, and repeatedly adding one unit to both sides, making sure the scale balances each time. (Note, however, that while one Base Ten long is equivalent in length to a row of ten units, it is not equivalent in weight to ten units. Therefore, dissuade children from trying to compare the weights of Base Ten Blocks having different values.)

Given sufficient time to explore, children will develop their own ways of estimating the number of units in a bag. Encourage them to look closely at the bags for visual clues. A child who has difficulty doing this may find using a benchmark of a given number of units to be helpful. Provide such a child with a bag of ten units. Encourage the child to handle and examine the bag of ten and then try to compare it to each of the other bags. Ask questions such as, "Which bag has more (or less)? Which has a few more (or a few less)? Which has many more (or many less)?"

In recording their handfuls of units on the *Weighing Numbers* worksheet, children are likely to write the greater number on the lower pan of the scale and the lesser number on the higher pan. Some children may record their

2. Encourage those children who are ready to compare greater numbers of units to do the activity again. This time, have them start by putting two or more handfuls of units into each bag.

data in number sentences. Others may even be ready to record inequalities. For example, to compare two handfuls, one of 30 units and the other of 17, children may write 30 − 17 = 13 and 17 + 13 = 30 or 30 > 17 and 17 < 30.

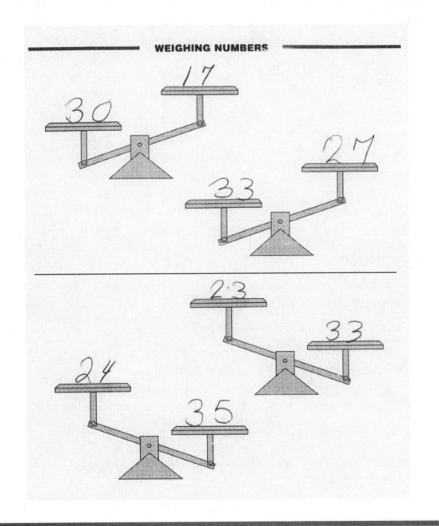

WEIGHING NUMBERS

BASE TEN BLOCKS BINGO

• Counting
• Place value
• Mental math

Getting Ready

What You'll Need

Base Ten Blocks, 1 set per group

Bingo Gameboards (10–50), 1 board per child, page 91

Bingo Gameboards (50–100), 1 board per child, page 92

Blank Bingo Gameboards, 1 board per child, page 93

Chips or counters, 6 per child

Overhead Base Ten Blocks and/or *Bingo Gameboards* transparencies (optional)

Overview

In this game for three or four players, children take turns picking groups of Base Ten Blocks and calling out the numbers they represent. Children cover the called numbers that appear on their gameboards in an effort to be the first to cover three numbers in a row. In this activity, children have the opportunity to:

◆ develop understanding of place value

◆ identify numbers to 50 or 100

The Activity

Point out that a gameboard has three rows, three columns, and two diagonals. Elicit that rows *go across the board*, columns *go up and down*, and diagonals *go from one corner to the opposite corner.*

You may wish to copy and distribute the gameboard that appears here on one of the outlines on the Blank Bingo Gameboards *BLM so that each child can circle the numbers as they are called.*

Introducing

◆ Write the numbers from 1 to 20 on individual slips of paper and put the slips into a bag.

◆ Copy this bingo gameboard on the chalkboard.

15	18	7
11	3	14
9	20	6

◆ Ask children if they have ever played bingo. Invite anyone who has to explain the game. Be sure everyone understands that players try to win this game by being first to cover all the numbers in one row, one column, or one diagonal on a gameboard.

◆ Demonstrate the game in this way. Explain that someone will pick a number from the bag and call it out. Children should raise their hands if they see that number on the gameboard.

◆ Designate a "Number Caller" to pick a number, announce it, and—if it is on the board—to call on someone to come up and circle it. (Once a slip has been picked, it should be set aside.)

◆ After children have circled several numbers and have come close to completing a row, column, and/or diagonal, remind them to be on the lookout for a "winning number."

◆ When a winning number is called and circled, ask children to tell whether the winning numbers form a row, a column, or a diagonal.

◆ Explain the rules given in *On Their Own* for *Base Ten Blocks Bingo*.

On Their Own

Play *Base 10 Blocks Bingo!*

Here are the rules.

1. This is a game for 3 or 4 players. The object is to be the first to cover 3 numbers in a row, column, or diagonal on gameboards like these.

50	25	11
18	38	40
46	29	21

16	28	30
37	13	48
19	42	26

26	44	31
22	12	36
50	49	16

47	39	19
20	17	44
15	35	33

2. Players each take 1 gameboard. They take turns being the Number Caller. The Number Caller makes up a number by:

   - picking 1, 2, 3, or 4 longs.
   - picking some units.
   - regrouping the units for a long if there are 10 or more units.
   - deciding what number the longs and units together represent.
   - calling out the number.

3. Everyone checks his or her board. Anyone with the number called covers it with a chip.

4. Whoever is first to cover 3 in a row *or* 3 in a column *or* 3 on a diagonal says "Bingo!" and wins the game.

- Exchange gameboards. Play *Base 10 Blocks Bingo* using your new board.

    Do this 2 more times.

- Be ready to tell about your games.

The Bigger Picture

Thinking and Sharing

Invite children to talk about their games and describe some of the thinking they did.

Use prompts like these to promote class discussion:

- How does the Number Caller have an advantage in this game?
- Do you think that all players have a fair chance of winning *Base Ten Blocks Bingo?* Explain.
- Did you ever realize that you had "Bingo" *after* someone else called it out? Explain.
- Is there any way to get better at playing this game? Explain.
- What else did you find out from playing the game?

Extending the Activity

1. Have children play the game again, but this time have them play in pairs instead of in groups, with each player using *two* bingo boards at once. To win this game, players must get three winning numbers on both cards.

2. Have groups play the game using the *Bingo Gameboards (50–100)*. The Number Caller for this game uses from five to nine longs and a handful of units to make up each number.

Teacher Talk

Where's the Mathematics?

Even when children seem to find rote counting to 50 or 100 to be easy, reading these numbers and modeling them may remain a great challenge. For example, some children who can count "...39, 40, 41, 42" may be unsure of whether to model 42 with four longs and two units or with two longs and four units. Other children may be able to write all the numbers from 1 to 100 in sequence and yet be unable to write them out of sequence, perhaps reversing the digits in some of them as they write. *Base Ten Blocks Bingo* helps correct these problems by motivating children to work at reading and modeling two-digit numbers.

The blocks help children to understand that the value of each digit in a two-digit number depends on its place in the number. When a Number Caller displays four longs and two units and then calls out "Forty-two," a child in the group who might otherwise be unsure of how to read "42" will immediately realize that the number of tens—represented by the longs—is read first in a number. (If the Number Caller reads a number that he or she has modeled incorrectly, be assured that the other members of the group will be quick to point out the error!)

If children have not yet learned to regroup, explain that if 10 or more units are picked for a number, 10 of them should be regrouped—or traded—for one long. If just a few children understand how to regroup, be sure to assign at least one of them to each playing group. And, whether or not children have mastered the regrouping process, suggest that they all check the Number Caller's regrouping to confirm that the blocks picked correctly represent the number called.

In addition to picking the blocks and making up the numbers, the Number Caller should also play the game. (If children seem to be confused by this, you may wish to act as Number Caller for the first few games.) Given the chance to both call and play, some Number Callers may be cunning enough to pick blocks that model numbers that they themselves need to win. If groups complain that their Number Callers are doing this and that it makes the game unfair, you may wish to suggest that the Number Caller for the next game does not also play.

With experience children will discover that other than being alert to the numbers being called out, there is no way to "get better at playing this

3. Challenge groups to work together to design their own bingo games using the *Blank Bingo Gameboards.*

game." Bingo is a game of chance, not a game of strategy, so everyone has an equal, or fair, chance of winning. Sometimes, however, when someone calls out "Bingo!" others then realize that they had already "won," having previously completed a winning row, column, or diagonal. Young children, newly accustomed to reading from left to right, sometimes identify *rows* of winning numbers but fail to recognize "wins" along columns or diagonals. For example, in the game shown, it was not until after Player A called out "Bingo!" that someone pointed out the unidentified win along the 15-17-19 diagonal on Player B's gameboard. Remind children to remain alert, not only by checking their gameboards for the new numbers being called but also by looking for patterns formed by the numbers they have covered.

If an overhead projector is available, you may want to have children use it to design their own gameboards. Make a transparency of the *Blank Bingo Gameboards* and make and distribute copies of these blank gameboards. Then divide the class into four teams. Designate one of the four gameboards on your transparency as belonging to each team. Call on children from each team to come up to the projector and write numbers on the transparency to create their gameboard. Meanwhile, other members of the team should record the numbers on their own boards. You may designate a class Number Caller or you may decide to be Number Caller yourself. Pick Base Ten longs and units and display them on the overhead. Children should work within their teams, modeling the blocks for themselves, and deciding whether or not they have a match to model on their boards. Keep a record of the numbers as you call them to later help check the teams' gameboards.

BUILD A BUG HOUSE

Getting Ready

What You'll Need

Base Ten Blocks (flats, longs, and units), 1 set per pair

Base Ten Blocks Place-Value Mat, 1 per child

Sticky notes

Drawing paper

Overview

Children build structures with Base Ten Blocks. They compare their structures by estimating the value of each. Then they count units to find the actual value of each structure and compare their counts to their estimates. In this activity, children have the opportunity to:

- ◆ determine the value of a group of blocks
- ◆ compare the values of various groups of blocks

The Activity

Introducing

- ◆ Build this structure with four flats. Tell children that this is your model of a doghouse. Have children copy it.

- ◆ Ask volunteers to tell what they notice about the structure.

- ◆ Elicit that the total value of the blocks that make up the doghouse is 400. Say that if doghouses had addresses, the address of this doghouse would be #400!

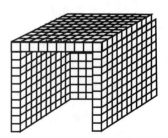

On Their Own

How can you use Base 10 Blocks to build a bug house?

- Work with a partner. Each of you take up to 16 blocks. You may take any combination of flats, longs, and units.

- Use all your blocks to build a bug house.

- Compare bug houses. Guess the value of each. The value is also the "address" of the bug house. Try to count the blocks without touching them to guess the address.

- Write the address on a sticky note. Carefully stick the address on the house.

- Draw a picture of your bug house.

- Now take your bug house apart. Put the blocks on a place-value mat.

- Find the value of the blocks on the mat. Trade blocks if you can. See if you guessed the address correctly.

- Do the activity again. This time, try to build a *better* bug house—maybe even a *bigger* bug house!

- Don't take this bug house apart. Leave it out where everyone can see it.

The Bigger Picture

Thinking and Sharing

Encourage children to walk around the room to observe all the bug houses. Tell them to look, but not to touch them. Suggest that children try to decide which bug houses are *the tallest, the shortest, the biggest,* and *the smallest.*

Use prompts like these to promote class discussion:

- How did you find the address of your bug house?

- When you took apart your bug house to check its address, did you need to trade blocks? Explain.

- Do the tallest (biggest) bug houses have the addresses with the greatest values? Explain.

- Do the shortest (smallest) bug houses have the addresses with the least values? Explain.

Drawing and Writing

Have children draw a bug that could live in one of their bug houses. Then have them tell why that house would make a good home for the bug.

Extending the Activity

1. Challenge children to build a bug house with a particular address, such as #256.

2. Have pairs compare their last two bug houses by determining which one has the greater address. Then tell children to add blocks to one of the houses or to take away blocks from one of them so that both houses have the same address.

Where's the Mathematics?

In determining the values, or "addresses," of their bug houses, children reinforce their understanding of the equivalent values of the Base Ten Blocks. They are repeatedly reminded, for example, that 1 flat is equivalent in value both to 10 longs and to 100 units. They begin to see why some groups of blocks can be exchanged, or traded, for others while still maintaining their original values.

As children initially compare their bug houses, they may merely notice differences in height and width and not in the numbers of the types of blocks used. Encourage them to look closely at each house, first to see which of the two houses contains the greater number of flats. If the houses contain the same number of flats, then children should compare to see which has the greater number of longs, and then the greater number of units.

You may want to have children record their guesses, or estimates, of the addresses at the top of a sticky note and later record the actual address (the actual value of the blocks) below it. This can lead to an informal comparison of the estimate with the actual count. The child whose work appears below, for example, estimated the address of his bug house to be 610. An actual count revealed the address to be 452. "The real address of my bug house is about 150 less than my guess!" the child announced.

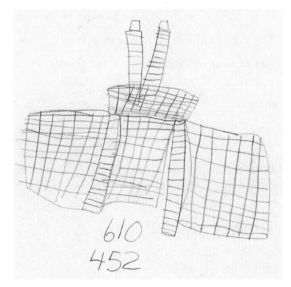

3. Tell children that a flea is a small insect about 1/8 in. (3 mm) long, and a tarantula is a large spider with a leg span that measures about 7 in. (18 cm) across. Record these measurements on the board. Then have one member of each pair use blocks to build a house for a flea while the other builds a house for a tarantula.

Some children may be reluctant to take their bug houses apart in order to determine the address. If you have an instant-picture camera available and can provide such children with snapshots of their bug houses, they may then become willing to take their structures apart in order to examine the component blocks.

After taking a bug house apart, children should sort their blocks by placing each kind in the corresponding column of a place-value mat, first counting the blocks in each column on the mat and then trading whenever possible. (Be sure that children understand how to trade each group of 10 units for 1 long and each group of 10 longs for 1 flat.) Then, point out that children should count the blocks with the greatest value (the flats), then count the longs, and then the units, counting by one hundreds, by tens, then by ones.

Developing a rationale for why a particular kind of bug is suited to "living" in their bug house is satisfying to children as it draws both on their sense of imagination and on their realization of cause and effect.

I think a bee would be perfed to live in the house because it is big endf to fit in the door and it can make alot of honey and I can fill the house up.

FEED THE BIRDS

- **Addition**
- **Subtraction**
- **Number relationships**

Getting Ready

What You'll Need

Base Ten units (20 per pair) and longs (10 per pair)

Feed the Birds workmat, 1 per child, page 94

Overhead Base Ten Blocks and/or *Feed the Birds* workmat transparency (optional)

Overview

Children use Base Ten units to model two addition facts and two related subtraction facts. In this activity, children have the opportunity to:

- ◆ represent the commutative property of addition
- ◆ explore the inverse relationship of addition and subtraction

The Activity

Introducing

- ◆ Invite three children to come to the front of the classroom. Have them count themselves aloud.
- ◆ Call up two more children. Tell them to count themselves.
- ◆ Record the action by writing this addition fact on the board: 3 + 2 = 5. Then have everyone return to their seats.
- ◆ Repeat the process, this time calling up two children first and then having three children join them. Record this on the board: 2 + 3 = 5.
- ◆ Establish that five children are at the front of the room. Then ask two of them to return to their seats. Record the subtraction fact for this action: 5 – 2 = 3.
- ◆ Now ask the two children who just sat down to rejoin the group of three. Then tell the three to return to their seats.
- ◆ Have a volunteer come to the board to record this action: 5 – 3 = 2.
- ◆ Lead a discussion about how the four number facts on the board are alike in some ways and different in others.

On Their Own

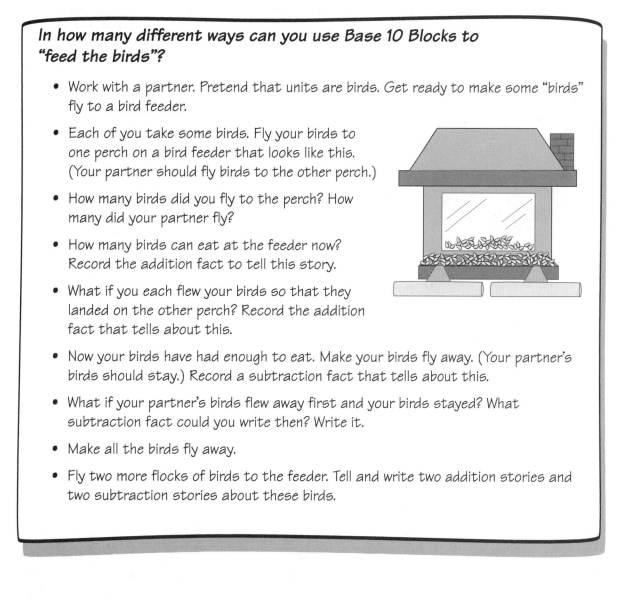

In how many different ways can you use Base 10 Blocks to "feed the birds"?

- Work with a partner. Pretend that units are birds. Get ready to make some "birds" fly to a bird feeder.

- Each of you take some birds. Fly your birds to one perch on a bird feeder that looks like this. (Your partner should fly birds to the other perch.)

- How many birds did you fly to the perch? How many did your partner fly?

- How many birds can eat at the feeder now? Record the addition fact to tell this story.

- What if you each flew your birds so that they landed on the other perch? Record the addition fact that tells about this.

- Now your birds have had enough to eat. Make your birds fly away. (Your partner's birds should stay.) Record a subtraction fact that tells about this.

- What if your partner's birds flew away first and your birds stayed? What subtraction fact could you write then? Write it.

- Make all the birds fly away.

- Fly two more flocks of birds to the feeder. Tell and write two addition stories and two subtraction stories about these birds.

The Bigger Picture

Thinking and Sharing

Call on pairs to tell how many birds they flew to their bird feeder. Have them come up to the board and record the addition and subtraction stories they identified for their two flocks of birds.

Use prompts like these to promote class discussion:

- How did you decide how many birds to fly to a perch?

- How are your addition stories like your subtraction stories? How are they different from your subtraction stories?

- Why could you write two addition stories for the same two flocks of birds?

- Why could you write two subtraction stories that start with the same number of birds?

Drawing and Writing

Have children draw birds on the perches of the bird feeder on a copy of the *Feed the Birds* workmat to represent the two flocks of birds that they and their partner "flew" to their feeder.

Extending the Activity

1. Have children repeat the activity using Snap™ Cubes or Color Tiles of two different colors to represent the two flocks of birds.

Teacher Talk

Where's the Mathematics?

Each pair of children will see the commutative property of addition come alive as they discover that they can write two addition number sentences for their two flocks of "birds." Young children are often surprised to find that the sum of the same two numbers remains the same regardless of the order in which they add them. Having them repeat the activity several times, perhaps using other manipulatives as birds, will further reinforce this understanding.

Feed the Birds also helps children to understand the inverse nature of the addition and subtraction operations. Children often learn the processes of addition and subtraction mechanically. This leaves them focusing on trying to remember the step-by-step procedures and not on what intuitively makes sense. Children are far more likely to come up with reasonable answers when they use concrete models to develop their understanding of number. The action of first combining two flocks of birds at a "feeder," then having one flock or the other "fly away" serves as a recognizable model of the addition and subtraction processes.

Distribute units alone for children's use as they begin this activity to lead them to model basic-fact families. Later, distribute longs so that children can model greater numbers, using each long to represent 10 birds. Some children may be ready to use both units and longs to model their flocks. The following number sentences were written by one pair that chose to "fly" 10 birds (1 long) to one side of the feeder and 21 birds (2 longs and 1 unit) to the other side.

$$10 + 21 = 31 \qquad 21 + 10 = 31$$
$$31 - 10 = 21 \qquad 31 - 21 = 10$$

2. Tell children to pretend that there are many more perches on both sides of the bird feeder. Have them repeat the activity, this time using longs instead of units, with each long representing 10 birds. For example, one partner may choose to fly 3 longs (30 birds) to the feeder while the other partner flies 5 longs (50 birds). Have children record related addition and subtraction sentences for these larger flocks of birds.

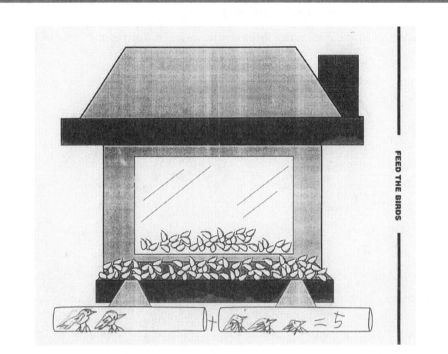

After children draw their birds to record how many flew to the feeder, (as shown above), ask them to suggest ways of using pictures to record how many birds flew away. Children may erase or cross out one flock or the other, or they may respond as one child did to this challenge—by holding up a blank worksheet and saying that it showed that *all* the birds had flown away!

HIDE AND DECIDE

Getting Ready

What You'll Need

Small paper grab bags, each containing 9 units and 9 (or fewer) longs, 1 bag per pair

Construction paper, 1 sheet per pair

1–100 Grid, 1 per pair, page 95

Clock or watch with second hand or a stopwatch

Overhead projector (optional)

Overhead Base Ten Blocks (optional)

Overview

Children get a glimpse of a group of Base Ten Blocks and then guess its value based on their recollection of what they saw. In this activity, children have the opportunity to:

- build visual imagery of numbers
- develop instant recognition of the value of a small quantity of blocks

The Activity

You may wish to have a volunteer keep track of the time, calling out "Begin" to signal the beginning of the viewing period and "Two seconds" to signal the end.

Introducing

- Out of children's sight, scatter five unit blocks and cover them with a sheet of paper. (Alternatively, if an overhead projector is available, arrange the units on the glass and then cover them with the paper.)
- Tell children that you have some Base Ten Blocks hidden under the paper and that you will give them a quick look at them. Warn children to be quiet about what they are about to see.
- Give a signal and then uncover the blocks for exactly two seconds.
- Cover the blocks again. Ask children to guess the value of the hidden blocks. Record some of their guesses. Encourage them to explain how they determined each amount.
- Uncover the blocks. Have children compare their guesses to the actual number of blocks that were hidden.
- Repeat this process several times, first hiding other numbers of units (up to ten) and then hiding a few units along with one or two longs.

On Their Own

Can you find the value of a group of Base 10 Blocks by taking 1 quick look?

- Work with a partner. Get a grab bag.
- Decide who will be the Grabber and who will be the Guesser.
- The Guesser turns away while the Grabber:
  - grabs a handful of blocks from the bag without looking.
  - covers the blocks with a sheet of paper.
- The Guesser gets ready to look.
- Now the Grabber:
  - uncovers the blocks for 2 seconds to let the Guesser look.
  - covers the blocks again.
- The Guesser tries to remember the blocks, makes a guess about their value, and records the guess.
- The Grabber uncovers the blocks. Together partners find their actual value.
- The Guesser marks the number that shows the actual value on a 1–100 grid. Then the Guesser compares the guess to the actual value.
- Do this activity again and again. Take turns being the Grabber and the Guesser.

1	2	3	4	5	6	7	8	9	10
11	12	13	14	15	16	17	18	19	20
21	22	23	24	25	26	27	28	29	30
31	32	33	34	35	36	37	38	39	40
41	42	43	44	45	46	47	48	49	50
51	52	53	54	55	56	57	58	59	60
61	62	63	64	65	66	67	68	69	70
71	72	73	74	75	76	77	78	79	80
81	82	83	84	85	86	87	88	89	90
91	92	93	94	95	96	97	98	99	100

The Bigger Picture

Thinking and Sharing

Have children talk about what happened as they worked through the activity.

Use prompts like these to promote class discussion:

- What was easy about this activity? What was hard?
- What could the Grabber do to make the activity easier or harder?
- When you were the Guesser, what did you think when you took a quick look at the blocks? Explain.
- When you were the Guesser, how well did you guess? Did your guesses get better when you did the activity again? Explain.

Writing

Tell children to pretend that they are all Guessers doing this activity. Have them describe how they would guess the value of the hidden blocks if they took a quick look and thought they saw five longs and four units.

Extending the Activity

Have children play a game called *Take a Quick Look.* Call on someone to be the Guesser. Have the Guesser stand at the back of the room facing

Teacher Talk

Where's the Mathematics?

Hide and Decide is intended to build children's sense of visual imagery. Even those young children who have not yet acquired the ability to count on from a given number will be eager to try to identify the number of blocks they see at a glance. The activity provides children with crucial practice in counting combinations of tens and ones and in counting on from multiples of tens.

Most children will be motivated by seeing their guesses become increasingly better as they repeat the activity. If any pairs find the activity to be so easy that their guesses continually match the actual values of the blocks, you may wish to increase the number of blocks in their bag. If, on the other hand, any pairs appear to be frustrated at not being able to improve their guesses, you may wish to have them work for a while with a bag that contains only units or only longs. Then, after having them do the activity for a while with just one kind of block, gradually add a few blocks of the other kind to their bag.

Some children have difficulty keeping track of what they have counted, recounting some already counted blocks and failing to count others. Encourage such children to touch each block as they count it, moving it to a new location with each count to strengthen their sense of one-to-one correspondence.

Explain that by making a guess, children are making an estimate, an answer that may not be exact. A quick look at the blocks followed by counting to find the actual value of the blocks will help children learn that good guesses or estimates are based on what they already know.

You may wish to suggest that children compare each guess with the exact answer by having the Grabber point to each number guessed on the 1–100 grid while the Guesser circles the actual value. Explain that sometimes a guess and its corresponding actual value are *far apart.* This means that there are many numbers between them. Other times a guess and its actual value are *close together.* This means that there are few numbers, or no numbers, between them. Be sure that children understand that their aim should always be to make a good guess, one that is close (or matching) in number to the actual value.

away from the class. Point to several children, silently signaling them to come up to form a group at the front of the room. Have the Guesser turn around to take a two-second look at the assembled group. Then, have him or her turn away again and guess the number of boys, the number of girls, and the total number in the group. Record the guesses. Have the Guesser turn around to check his or her guesses and then choose the next Guesser.

1–100 GRID

1	2	3	4	5	6	7	8	9	10
11	12	13	14	15	16	17	18	19	20
21	22	23	24	25	26	27	28	29	30
31	32	33	34	35	36	37	38	39	40
41	42	43	44	45	46	47	48	49	50
51	52	53	54	55	56	57	58	59	60
61	62	63	64	65	66	67	68	69	70
71	72	73	74	75	76	77	78	79	80
81	82	83	84	85	86	87	88	89	90
91	92	93	94	95	96	97	98	99	100

Have children continue the activity either for a given length of time or until they have marked most of the numbers on their 1–100 grid. If you have filled the grab bags with different numbers of blocks, you may wish to have pairs exchange bags after a while. Later, ask children to tell what differences they notice in the numbers they grab using the new bags.

Children's explanations of how they thought about the blocks they glimpsed provides interesting insights into their level of mathematical thinking. One first grader, when asked to describe what she was thinking after taking a quick look at what appeared to be five longs and four units wrote:

> I counted the big longs 10, 20, 30, 40, 50 and then I counted the little ones 51, 52, 53, 54. I couldn't count quick enough because I was still counting even though I couldn't see through the paper I just kept counting the squares.

HOW MANY CAN YOU HOLD?

- Counting
- Estimation

Getting Ready

What You'll Need

Base Ten Blocks, 1 set per pair

1–100 Grid, 1 per pair, page 95

Plastic containers of various sizes (optional)

Overview

Children estimate and then count the number of Base Ten units that they can hold in their two hands. In this activity, children have the opportunity to:

- ◆ make and revise estimates
- ◆ use place-value concepts
- ◆ explore capacity

The Activity

Introducing

- ◆ Grab a large handful of units in one hand. Now display the handful and ask children to guess, or estimate, the number of units you are holding.

- ◆ Have children each write a secret estimate on a piece of paper. Tell them to fold the papers to hide the estimates.

- ◆ Now have children count along with you as you place each unit, one to a box, on a 1–100 grid. About halfway through the count, ask children to think about their estimates. If they would now like to change their estimates, allow them to write a second estimate next to their first.

- ◆ Finish counting the blocks. Invite children to each compare their own estimate(s) with the number on which the last unit was placed.

- ◆ Have children tell whether their estimate was close to the actual number of units. Ask those children who made a second estimate whether or not it was closer than their first.

On Their Own

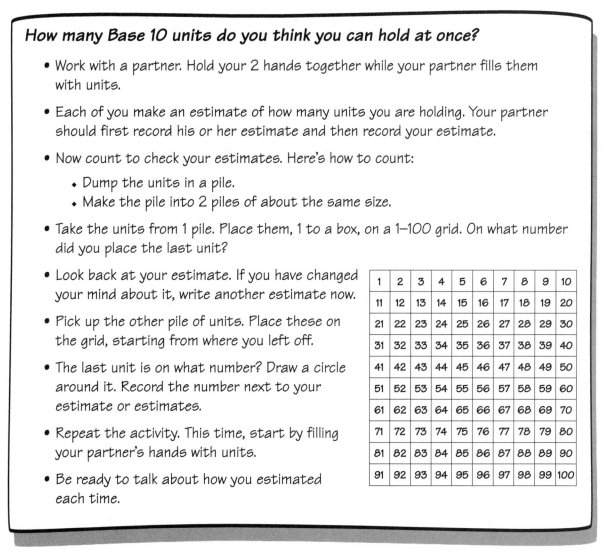

How many Base 10 units do you think you can hold at once?

- Work with a partner. Hold your 2 hands together while your partner fills them with units.

- Each of you make an estimate of how many units you are holding. Your partner should first record his or her estimate and then record your estimate.

- Now count to check your estimates. Here's how to count:
  - Dump the units in a pile.
  - Make the pile into 2 piles of about the same size.

- Take the units from 1 pile. Place them, 1 to a box, on a 1–100 grid. On what number did you place the last unit?

- Look back at your estimate. If you have changed your mind about it, write another estimate now.

- Pick up the other pile of units. Place these on the grid, starting from where you left off.

- The last unit is on what number? Draw a circle around it. Record the number next to your estimate or estimates.

- Repeat the activity. This time, start by filling your partner's hands with units.

- Be ready to talk about how you estimated each time.

1	2	3	4	5	6	7	8	9	10
11	12	13	14	15	16	17	18	19	20
21	22	23	24	25	26	27	28	29	30
31	32	33	34	35	36	37	38	39	40
41	42	43	44	45	46	47	48	49	50
51	52	53	54	55	56	57	58	59	60
61	62	63	64	65	66	67	68	69	70
71	72	73	74	75	76	77	78	79	80
81	82	83	84	85	86	87	88	89	90
91	92	93	94	95	96	97	98	99	100

The Bigger Picture

Thinking and Sharing

Invite pairs to talk about what happened each time they worked through the activity.

Use prompts like these to promote class discussion:

- How did you decide on your first estimate?

- After you counted about half the units, did you change your estimate? Explain.

- The second time you did the activity were your estimates closer to the actual number of units? Explain.

- What is meant by a "good estimate"?

Writing

Bring the largest pair of adult-size gloves you can find to class. Have one child put them on and use both hands to scoop up as many units as possible. Have children describe how they would go about estimating the number of units being held. After children finish writing, count the units aloud with them so that they can check their estimates.

Where's the Mathematics?

How Many Can You Hold? helps sharpen children's number sense by leading them to think about the reasonableness of their answers. Challenging children to made estimates and then evaluate whether or not their estimates make sense helps to reinforce the idea that we should approximate numerical amounts based on what we know and not on "wild" guesses.

After filling one partner's hands with unit blocks, each member of a pair should estimate the total number of units independently. To ensure that each partner's estimate reflects his or her own thinking, have the partner doing the recording secretly record his or her own estimate first and then ask for and record the other child's estimate.

Some children may sight the filled hands, realize that they contain a great many units, and then go on to "estimate" that there are 100, 1,000, or even 1,000,000 units! Finding an actual count for about half the total number of units sheds light on the estimation process. After counting the first half of the units, many children will be able to generalize how they should change their estimates to more accurately estimate the entire quantity.

Make sure that children understand that the purpose of changing an estimate after counting about half of the units is to make a *better* estimate, one that is probably closer to the actual value of the total. It is important that children understand that a good estimate should be close in number to the actual value while not necessarily matching it exactly. Encourage children to state their estimates in approximate terms as, for example, "about 15" or "between 20 and 24."

After children have distributed the units in their first pile, remind them to look carefully at the units that remain in the second pile in order to help them improve their estimates. One child described how he did this by explaining that he looked back and forth between the 1–100 grid and the

Extending the Activity

Challenge children to estimate how many units containers of different sizes can hold. After having children fill containers of different sizes with units, tell them to count about half of the contents. At this point, allow them to decide whether or not to make a better estimate. Have children complete their counts and compare their estimate(s) to their final counts.

---

remaining pile of units trying to imagine how many more units were in that pile and where the last one would end up if they were counted out onto the grid. The child wrote:

> You look at the blocks and you look at the paper and amagin how many there are.

Do not hesitate to be creative as you lead children to understand the process of estimating. One teacher's search for large adult-size gloves led her to a pair of huge rubber gloves. Because the children in her class had begun the activity with a set of Base Ten Blocks containing 100 units, they knew there could be no more than 100 units in any pair of hands at one time. The teacher thought of a fanciful model that would skew the activity in such a way that would distract the children from focusing on the fact that they had a maximum of 100 units. Out of sight of the class, the teacher spilled the units into one of the large gloves, pushing them down into each of the fingers and then filling the glove to the top. This glove provided an exciting challenge that inspired the children to estimate the number of units in this special "handful"!

LOOKING FOR LENGTH

- **Estimation**
- **Counting**
- **Measuring**
- **Comparing**

Getting Ready

What You'll Need

Base Ten Blocks, 1 long and 20 units per pair

Small paper bags, 1 per pair

Looking for Length worksheet, 1 per pair, page 96

Overview

Children envision the length of a Base Ten long to help them estimate the lengths of various classroom objects. They record their estimates, measure the objects with Base Ten units, and then compare their estimates to the actual measurements. In this activity, children have the opportunity to:

◆ estimate measurements

◆ collect data

◆ recognize that units and longs represent standard units of measure

The Activity

Explain that another name for the length of a Base Ten unit is 1 centimeter (1 cm). Since children know that 10 units are equal in length to 1 long, they should be able to understand why another name for 1 long is 10 centimeters (10 cm).

Introducing

◆ Distribute pencils of various lengths, one to a child.

◆ Ask children to estimate the length of their pencils in terms of Base Ten units.

◆ Set up a chalkboard chart like the one below and have several volunteers come to the board to record their estimates only.

NAME	LENGTH OF PENCIL	
	Estimate	Actual
	____ units	____ units
	____ units	____ units

◆ Distribute handfuls of units. Show children how to line up units along the length of their pencils starting from one end. Point out that the units should be touching, with no spaces between them.

◆ Have children announce the length of each pencil by saying, "My pencil is ____ units long" or "My pencil is *about* ____ units long."

◆ Have those volunteers who recorded their estimates on the board return to write the actual measurements. (Suggest that children whose pencils are shorter or longer than a whole number of units insert the word "about" before the closest whole number of units.)

On Their Own

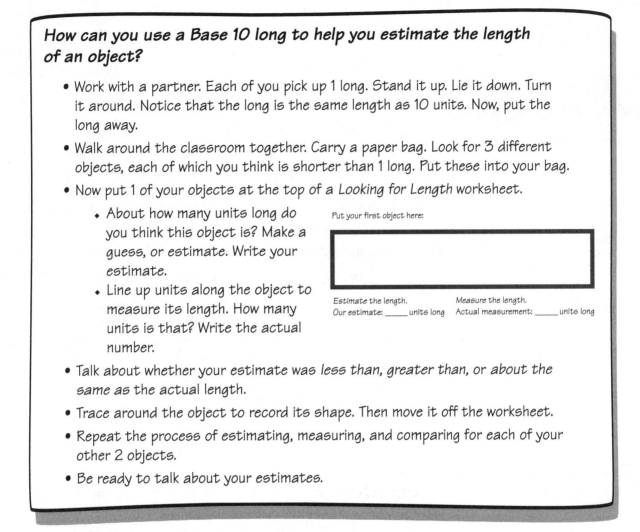

How can you use a Base 10 long to help you estimate the length of an object?

- Work with a partner. Each of you pick up 1 long. Stand it up. Lie it down. Turn it around. Notice that the long is the same length as 10 units. Now, put the long away.

- Walk around the classroom together. Carry a paper bag. Look for 3 different objects, each of which you think is shorter than 1 long. Put these into your bag.

- Now put 1 of your objects at the top of a *Looking for Length* worksheet.

    - About how many units long do you think this object is? Make a guess, or estimate. Write your estimate.
    - Line up units along the object to measure its length. How many units is that? Write the actual number.

    Put your first object here:

    Estimate the length.
    Our estimate: _____ units long

    Measure the length.
    Actual measurement: _____ units long

- Talk about whether your estimate was *less than, greater than,* or *about the same as* the actual length.

- Trace around the object to record its shape. Then move it off the worksheet.

- Repeat the process of estimating, measuring, and comparing for each of your other 2 objects.

- Be ready to talk about your estimates.

The Bigger Picture

Thinking and Sharing

Have pairs cut apart their worksheets along the dotted lines. Call them up to the board to post their recordings in three columns according to the actual lengths of their objects: Shorter Than 10 Cm, Equal to 10 Cm, and Longer Than 10 Cm.

Use prompts like these to promote class discussion:

- What makes an estimate good? What makes an estimate less good?

- Which of your estimates were good? Explain.

- Were you ever unsure about which side of an object to measure? How did you decide?

- Did measuring one object ever help you estimate the length of another? Explain.

Some children will have difficulty differentiating between the length and width of certain objects whose dimensions are close in number. If this is the case, point out that children can decide for themselves which side of the object to call the length.

Extending the Activity

1. Have pairs repeat the activity, this time challenging them to find three objects each of which is shorter than *2 longs* placed end to end.

Teacher Talk

Where's the Mathematics?

The challenge of aligning one side of an object to be measured with one end of a measuring tool seems insurmountable to many children. This activity provides the necessary time for children to focus on how to position objects in order to measure them without requiring the children to also focus on reading the scale on a ruler in order to determine length.

Some children find the lining up of an object with the measuring tool to be easiest if they put the object on the floor and then push it up against the wall "until it can't go any more." Just placing a Base Ten long on the floor next to the object in the same way creates the proper alignment for measuring. Children can then readily judge whether the object is shorter or longer than 1 long. If it appears to be shorter, then they count the number of units on the long from the point at which it and the object touch the wall to the point at which the object ends. If the object appears to be longer, then they add on units to the free end of the long until they have created a customized measuring tool of about the same length as the object. At this point, children must employ the process of counting on.

Some children may begin measuring objects that are longer than 1 long by first counting the (10) individual units within the long and then counting on, 1 count for each additional unit affixed to the end of the long. After doing this many times, some children will realize that each long represents a count of 10, and so they will begin to measure objects longer than 1 long by saying "10," and then immediately counting on, "...11, 12, 13,...."

2. Have the entire class pool the objects they collected and sort them according to their actual lengths, from shortest to longest. Encourage children to develop a way to make a class record of these findings.

Perspective plays a vital role in measuring length. Because of this, *Looking for Length* encourages children to examine a long as they position and then re-position it in different ways. This is done because sometimes children are more successful at envisioning length as a horizontal measurement, whereas at other times they are better able to envision it as a vertical measurement.

Put your third object here:

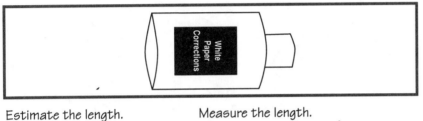

Estimate the length.   Measure the length.
Our estimate: __8__ units long   Actual measurement: __6__ units long

It is likely that most of the objects children collect in their bags will not be equal in length to an exact number of units. Suggest that children use words such as "about ____ units long" or "a little less than (more than) ____ units long" to report the lengths of these objects. If some children understand that a fraction or a decimal represents part of a number, they may report the length of an object to be, for example, "6 and a half units" or "6.5 cm."

MAKING PATTERNS

- Making patterns
- Pattern recognition
- Sorting and classifying

Getting Ready

What You'll Need

Base Ten Blocks

Classroom objects (3 or 4 of each of several different kinds)

Base Ten Block Grid Paper, 1 sheet per child, page 109

Overhead Base Ten Blocks (optional)

Overview

Children use Base Ten Blocks to build and repeat patterns. They analyze their partners' patterns and extend them. In this activity, children have the opportunity to:

◆ notice likenesses and differences between patterns

◆ use letters to identify patterns

The Activity

If children have difficulty seeing how each sequence in the pattern repeats, put rulers on the table to separate each sequence from the next.

Introducing

- ◆ Use two kinds of classroom objects (a crayon and a book, for example) as the core of a pattern.

- ◆ Build the pattern on a table making sure it repeats several times. Show, for example, crayon, book; crayon, book; crayon, book; crayon, book.

- ◆ Ask children to describe how the pattern begins. They may say, for example, "crayon, book" or "little, big" or "write with it, read it."

- ◆ Establish that in this pattern two things together keep repeating, first one and then the other. Say that an easy way to describe a pattern like this is with the letters *A* and *B,* each of which stands for one of the objects.

- ◆ Call on volunteers to change the pattern by adding other objects to create an *ABB* pattern and then an *ABC* pattern. Discuss how the letters in each pattern represent different objects that repeat in a predictable way.

On Their Own

How can you use Base 10 Blocks to make a pattern that repeats?

- Work by yourself. Look at these patterns. See how they repeat.

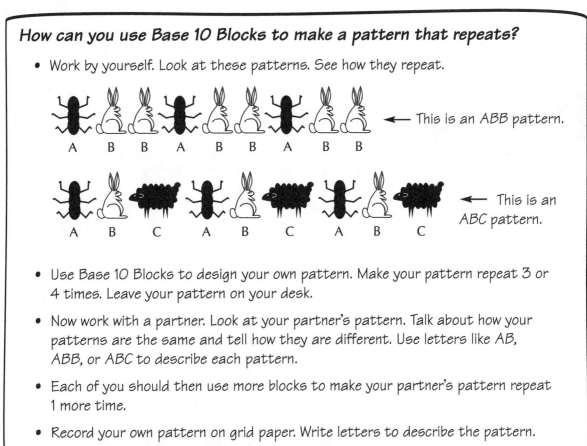

← This is an ABB pattern.

A B B A B B A B B

← This is an ABC pattern.

A B C A B C A B C

- Use Base 10 Blocks to design your own pattern. Make your pattern repeat 3 or 4 times. Leave your pattern on your desk.

- Now work with a partner. Look at your partner's pattern. Talk about how your patterns are the same and tell how they are different. Use letters like AB, ABB, or ABC to describe each pattern.

- Each of you should then use more blocks to make your partner's pattern repeat 1 more time.

- Record your own pattern on grid paper. Write letters to describe the pattern.

The Bigger Picture

Thinking and Sharing

Write these pattern designations—*AB, ABB,* and *ABC* —as column headings across the chalkboard. Invite children to post their patterns below the corresponding headings. Draw children's attention to the different Base Ten Blocks patterns within each column.

Use prompts like these to promote class discussion:

- Why do you think that there are so many different kinds of patterns in each column?

- How are the patterns of each kind alike? How are they different?

- How could you describe your pattern without using letters?

- How does reading a pattern aloud help you to know what comes next?

Drawing

Have children use grid paper to show two more patterns they can make with just longs and units. Have them label the objects in each pattern with A's, B's, and C's to show how the pattern repeats.

Teacher Talk

Where's the Mathematics?

This activity gives children practice in recognizing, describing, and repeating patterns and in creating patterns of their own. Once they succeed in developing Base Ten Blocks patterns, children can go on to apply patterning concepts to the identification of number patterns.

Probably the most important concept that children should learn from this work is that a pattern begins with a core, or basic, design. The core design repeats over and over again to form the actual pattern.

Some children may struggle to identify the core design of a pattern. They may be able to name the two or three elements that make up the core and yet fail to recognize the importance of determining the exact order in which the elements occur, from left to right. Describing the first few elements of the pattern in words can be helpful in reinforcing the notion of left-to-right (or first-to-last) order. Sometimes, having children perform a repeated action, such as clap hands/clap hands/touch knees, will help them in identifying the core. Challenging children to circle or underline the core design of a pattern that another child recorded can also help.

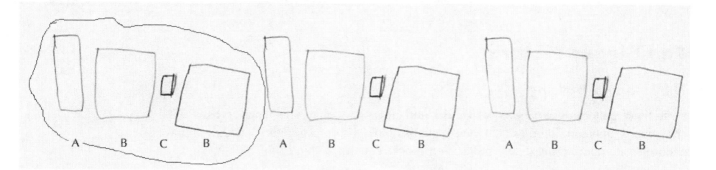

Children's first efforts are likely to be *AB* patterns based on very elementary core designs. As they create additional patterns, their work may reflect pattern schemes such as *ABC* and *AABB,* examples of which follow.

Extending the Activity

Challenge children to "translate" one of their patterns into colors, pictures, and sounds. For example, the *AAB* pattern of unit, unit, long could be translated as red, red, yellow; as dog, dog, cat; or as snap, snap, clap.

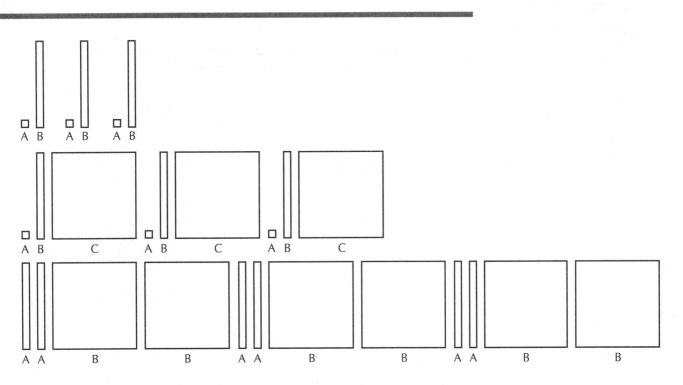

Once their patterns are posted, children can see that a variety of different patterns can reflect the same scheme. Any children having difficulty discerning likenesses and differences between two patterns may benefit from placing the patterns side by side in order to compare them.

Various classroom materials can provide children with a seemingly unending supply of patterning materials. One child successfully translated her *AABBB* block pattern (unit, unit, long, long, long) into the pattern shown below through the use of two rubber stamps, a stamp pad, and a long strip of paper.

MAKING RECTANGLES

- Shape recognition
- Spatial visualization
- Counting
- Properties of geometric shapes
- Area

Getting Ready

What You'll Need

Base Ten Blocks, 1 set per pair

Base Ten Block Grid Paper, 1 sheet per child, page 109

Overhead Base Ten Blocks (optional)

Overview

Children try to make as many different rectangles as possible with 12 Base Ten unit blocks. In this activity, children have the opportunity to:

- ◆ understand the attributes of rectangles
- ◆ realize that a rectangle's orientation does not affect its size or shape
- ◆ explore the concept of area

The Activity

Introducing

- ◆ Ask children to tell what they know about rectangles.
- ◆ Draw a rectangle on the chalkboard. Count the sides and the corners aloud with the class.
- ◆ Tell children to each use 6 units to form a rectangle. Then guide them to count the units to confirm that there are 6.
- ◆ Call on a volunteer to describe his or her rectangle.
- ◆ Ask someone else to describe a rectangle that looks different even though it has the same number of rows and the same number of units in each row as does the first volunteer's rectangle.
- ◆ Be sure that children understand that two rectangles can be the same, even though they are oriented differently.

On Their Own

How many different rectangles can you make using 12 unit blocks?

- Work with a partner. Get ready to make rectangles with units.

- Count out 12 units.

- Use all 12 units to make a rectangle.

- Talk about this rectangle with your partner.

- Record your rectangle on grid paper.

- Have your partner record it in a different way.

- Use the same 12 units to make a different rectangle. Record it in 2 ways.

- Keep on making and recording different 12-unit rectangles until you have made as many as you can.

- Be ready to talk about your work.

The Bigger Picture

Thinking and Sharing

Invite one pair to display the recordings they made of one of their rectangles and describe them while the other children check to see if they recorded the same ones. Ask another pair to display a different 12-unit rectangle. Continue until all possible 12-unit rectangles are on display.

Use prompts like these to promote class discussion:

- How many different 12-unit rectangles did you find?

- How are your rectangles the same? How are they different?

- How could you turn one of your rectangles to show a different rectangle?

- How can you describe a rectangle by its number of rows and the number of units in each row?

Writing

Have children use words, numbers, and pictures to tell how some rectangles made with 12 Base Ten blocks are alike and how some are different.

You may want to point out that a square is a special kind of rectangle. A square has four square corners like other rectangles. But, unlike other rectangles, all four sides of a square are the same length.

Extending the Activity

1. Have pairs repeat the activity, this time using *16* units instead of 12 to make their rectangles.

Where's the Mathematics?

Making Rectangles develops children's spatial sense and number sense as it requires them to make different rectangles from the same number of unit blocks. The activity also offers children an informal introduction to the commutative property of multiplication when, for example, it has them compare a 3-by-4 rectangle with a 4-by-3 rectangle and describe how the two are alike in some ways and different in others.

Children will use a variety of descriptions to compare their 12-unit rectangles. One boy described one of the rectangles that he and his partner made in this way.

It has 12 boxes.

It has 4 corners.

They're even. One side's even and the other side's even.

When it goes this way, it makes 4 wide and when it goes the other way, it is 3 wide.

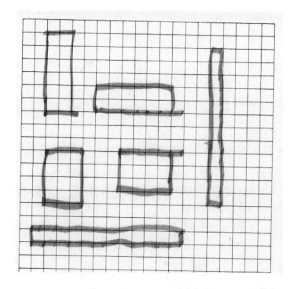

The same child then counted the three rows of this rectangle by fours: "4, 8, 12." Then he carefully turned the rectangle, keeping the configuration intact, and counted the four rows by threes: "3, 6, 9, 12." "See," he said. "It's the same both ways...sort of!"

2. Have children create any geometric shape using twelve units. Talk about how each of these shapes is like and/or different from their 12-unit rectangles.

In describing his 6-by-2 rectangle, the same boy announced that it had "more units on each side" than did his 3-by-4 rectangle. Then he pointed out that he could "...move two of the sets of three from the 3-by-4 rectangle and put them below the other two sets of three to make it look like this 6-by-2 rectangle."

Many children will fail to identify the 1-by-12 (12-by-1) rectangle. One girl started building this rectangle by lining up a single row of units. She stopped before adding the last few units, telling her teacher that this wouldn't be a rectangle because it had only two sides. Eventually, the child decided that the row of 12 units did form a rectangle, but she never seemed to feel very sure about it!

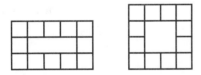

Some children may use their 12 units to form these open rectangles.

If children display these rectangles, ask them how many units they would need to fill each of the open spaces. Have them actually fill them in with units. Then ask them to identify the number of units that make up each new (filled-in) rectangle.

Building 16-unit rectangles will provide children with reinforcement of what they have already learned but with the added surprise of producing the special kind of rectangle that has the same number of units on all four sides—the square. Children will be quick to point out that this rectangle looks exactly the same, no matter how they turn it!

NUMBER BUILDER

Getting Ready

What You'll Need

Base Ten Blocks, 1 set per pair
Large books or boxes to use as barriers
Overhead Base Ten Blocks (optional)

Overview

Children use Base Ten Blocks to build secret numbers. Then they give clues about their secret numbers that their partners can use to try to build them. In this activity, children have the opportunity to:

- ◆ use place-value vocabulary
- ◆ identify two- and three-digit numbers
- ◆ communicate specific information

The Activity

Introducing

- ◆ Build any two-digit number with Base Ten Blocks and have children do the same.

- ◆ Tell children to think about what clues they could give to someone who can't see the blocks about the number or about the blocks used to build it.

- ◆ Call on volunteers to suggest clues. Record the clues on the chalkboard. For example, suppose you built the number 86 with 8 longs and 6 units. Children might give these clues.

  It has 8 tens and 6 ones.
  It has 14 blocks.
  It is less than 100.
  It is greater than 50.
  It is an even number.
  It is between 80 and 90.

- ◆ Ask children to identify any clues that are too general or that might be confusing.

- ◆ Try to get a consensus about which clues best describe your number.

On Their Own

How can you build a secret number with Base 10 Blocks and then describe it so that your partner can build it too?

- Work with a partner. Put up a big book or box between you.

- Decide who will be the first Number Builder.

- The Number Builder:
  - secretly chooses some flats, longs, and units.
  - uses these blocks to build a secret number.
  - gives clues to help the partner build the secret number.

- The partner follows the clues and builds a number. Then, both partners check to see if the numbers match.

- Take turns being the Number Builder.

- Here is an example. These blocks show a secret number. See how the clues tell about the number.

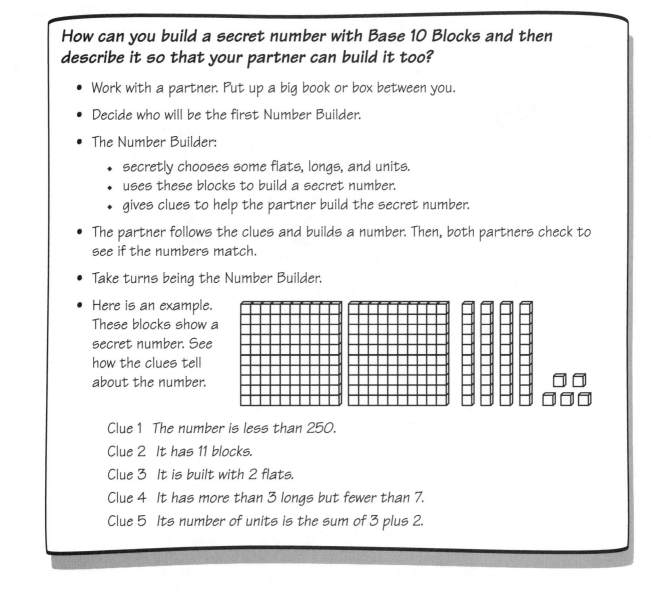

  Clue 1 The number is less than 250.
  Clue 2 It has 11 blocks.
  Clue 3 It is built with 2 flats.
  Clue 4 It has more than 3 longs but fewer than 7.
  Clue 5 Its number of units is the sum of 3 plus 2.

The Bigger Picture

Thinking and Sharing

Invite pairs to discuss their experiences in giving clues and in following them. Have some pairs draw the blocks they used for one of their secret numbers on the chalkboard. They can draw ■ for flats, | for longs, and • for units.

Use prompts like these to promote class discussion:

- What were some of your best clues? What made them so good?

- Why were some of the numbers easier to build from clues than other numbers?

- Which of your secret numbers was the easiest to give clues for? Which was the hardest? Explain.

- What kinds of clues were the most helpful?

Writing and Drawing

Have children use words, numbers, and pictures to record the clues they gave for one of their secret numbers.

Where's the Mathematics?

Logical thinking is closely related to language development. This activity gives children experience in listening to and creating mathematical language. Children use this language to apply deductive reasoning both in making up a good set of clues and in analyzing their partner's clues. *Number Builder* challenges children to interpret and combine bits of information toward a goal—that of discovering their partners' secret numbers. For example, if a child's first clue states that her secret number has no flats, her partner should be able to reason that the number is probably less than 100. If her second clue states that the number includes five longs, then her partner can be sure that the number falls anywhere from 50 to 59.

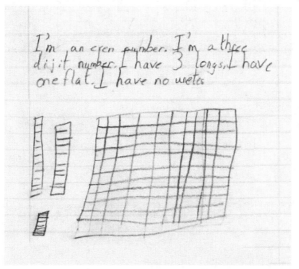

Formulating accurate clues may be too great a challenge for some young children. Such children will benefit from a whole-class version of the activity in which a designated Number Builder models a number with Base Ten Blocks on the overhead projector. The class can discuss which blocks and how many of each make up the number. You may wish to restate each bit of information a child offers in the form of a clue, identifying it as such. For example, if a child points out that he counted 13 blocks in the secret number, you might say, "The first clue is 'It has 13 blocks'" as you record the clue on the board.

After observing several pairs' work, one teacher decided to provide children with bags of unspecified numbers of Base Ten Blocks from which to build their secret numbers. This was because she had noticed that a few children were able to immediately identify their partners' secret numbers even without hearing a single clue. These children had counted the blocks of each kind that remained in the bag that held the familiar set once their partners had removed some blocks. While this process showed children's ingenuity (as well their subtraction prowess), it did little to further their clue-writing and clue-solving abilities!

Extending the Activity

Have children repeat the activity using the same secret numbers they used at first. But this time, they should build the numbers using different numbers of blocks. For example, someone who first built the number 329 with 3 flats, 2 longs, and 9 units might now build it with 2 flats, 11 longs, and 19 units.

After building their secret numbers, children will go about developing their own clues in different ways. At first, they may give one or two clues that tell too much, or even give away their numbers, leaving little to their partners' imaginations. With experience, though, children create clues that offer smaller bits of information. They realize that good clues are those which build upon one another, leading from the general to the specific.

One member of a pair reported that the most helpful clues were "...clues about two digits because they tell that the secret number is smaller than 100." The other partner said that clues about two digits were helpful because "...you know it means the number is 10 or higher."

Some children may deliberately offer misinformation to keep their partners from guessing their number too quickly. (If you become aware of children doing this, point out that a clue must give only true information about the secret number.)

Children enjoy the challenge of representing their secret numbers in different ways. A stamp pad and a set of Base Ten Blocks rubber stamps provided one child with an easy way to record two variations of her secret number, 121.

> If it has 2 digits the number is betwen 10-99. If the number is 7 it is 1 digit if the number is 100 it is 3 digit.

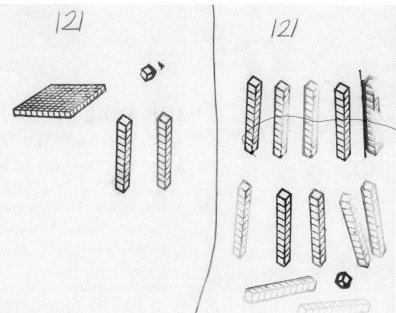

RACE FOR A FLAT

Getting Ready

What You'll Need

Base Ten Blocks, 1 set per group

Base Ten Blocks Place-Value Mat, 1 per pair

Number cubes marked 1 to 6, 2 per group

Units/Longs Spinner, 1 per pair, page 97

Overhead Base Ten Blocks (optional)

Overview

In this game for two pairs of children, players take turns rolling number cubes and finding the sums of the numbers rolled. They take Base Ten Blocks to represent the sums in an effort to be the first to accumulate blocks with a total value of 100. In this activity, children have an opportunity to:

◆ develop understanding of place value

◆ count on by ones

◆ add mentally

◆ regroup, or "trade," units (ones) for longs (tens)

The Activity

Introducing

◆ Go over the game rules for *Race for a Flat.*

◆ Invite two volunteers to play part of a demonstration game with you. (You may wish to play until someone gets blocks worth 50.)

◆ Each player should have a place-value mat. You go first.

◆ On your first turn, announce the sum of the digits you roll. If the sum was 10 or more, point out that you must trade 10 units for 1 long.

◆ After your second turn, point out that the blocks on your mat are from your first and second turns combined.

◆ Play until each player has had several turns. Tell the rest of the class to call out "Trade!" whenever 10 units should be traded for 1 long.

On Their Own

Play *Race for a Flat!*

Here are the rules.

1. This is a game for 2 teams of 2 players each. The object is to get enough longs and units to trade for a flat worth 100.

2. One team rolls 2 number cubes. The players find the sum of the numbers they roll and take units to show that number. Then they put their units on a place-value mat.

3. If the team gets 10 units or more, it trades 10 units for 1 long.

4. Teams take turns rolling, finding the sum, putting units on their mats, and trading units for longs.

5. As soon as a team gets blocks worth 100 or more, it makes a trade for 1 flat. The first team to do this wins.

- Clear your mats. Now play again.

- Be ready to talk about what you did to get a flat.

The Bigger Picture

Thinking and Sharing

Invite children to talk about their games and describe some of the thinking they did.

Use prompts like these to promote class discussion:

- ◆ After you rolled the number cubes, how did you know how many units to put on your mat?

- ◆ If your first roll was a five and a six, what would you put on your mat? Explain.

- ◆ How did you decide when to trade units for longs?

- ◆ What was the greatest sum you could get on one roll of two number cubes? When could rolling that sum help you win the game?

Drawing and Writing

Have children pretend that they have blocks worth 93 on their place-value mat. Tell them to draw blocks with a value of 93 on the mat. Then tell them that they may have one more roll. Have them figure out which numbers they could roll to reach 100 or more on their next turn.

Extending the Activity

Have pairs of teams play an alternative version of the game using just one number cube and the *Units/Longs Spinner.* Each team rolls and spins, and

Teacher Talk

Where's the Mathematics?

Although children may know how to count to 100, they sometimes have difficulty in bridging the decades—that is, in continuing the counting from one decade to the next. For example, when counting "...56, 57, 58, 59..." a child may fail to remember that 60 comes next in the sequence and may instead name some other multiple of ten. *Race for a Flat* reinforces children's understanding of the order in which numbers are sequenced from one decade to the next.

Observe how children determine their sums when they roll the number cubes. Upon seeing the numbers rolled, some children will immediately identify the basic number fact they represent and name the sum. Others will find the sum in different ways, perhaps using units to count one to one or using their fingers to keep track of the count. Notice whether children begin by counting each number individually and then recount the two together or whether they count on from one number through the next. In other words, if a pair rolls 4 and 6, notice whether children count "1, 2, 3, 4" and "1, 2, 3, 4, 5, 6" and then recount all from 1 to 10 or whether they recognize that they can count on starting with 5 or with 7. While any method children use for determining the sums should be acceptable, children's various methods reflect their differing levels of progress.

You may want to allow any children who seem to be having difficulty finding sums to play the game with just one number cube. Most children, though, will have no trouble readily recording each turn as an addition fact and keeping a running total until they reach 100 or more. After various rounds, you may wish to challenge teams to compare their blocks with those of their opponents and tell whose blocks represent the greater number.

Through the process of adding blocks to their mats for successive rolls, children's counting and trading abilities should strengthen. To find each new sum, children may count on from the blocks already on their mats. For

then puts the number of blocks rolled of the kind spun on their mat. Again, teams play until they can trade their units and/or longs for a flat.

example, consider a pair that has on its mat 3 longs and 8 units (for a total of 38). If the pair then rolls a 3, children may simply count on, "...39, 40, 41." Instead of adding 3 units to the 8 already in the units column on their mat and then trading 10 units for a long, children may directly add one long to the mat and remove all but one of the units.

Pay particular attention to children's explanations of how they determined that the greatest sum that they can roll on two number cubes, 12, could help them to win the game at the point at which they had a total of 88 or more. Do children realize that 88 plus 12 would bring them to exactly 100 and enable them to trade for a flat? Do they realize that a roll of 12 (units) added to any total greater than 88 would bring them beyond 100?

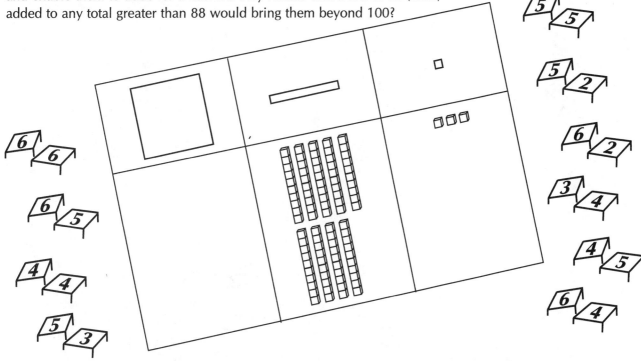

RACE TO CLEAR THE MAT

Getting Ready

What You'll Need

Base Ten Blocks, 1 set per group

Base Ten Blocks Place-Value Mat, 1 per child

Number cubes marked 1 to 6, 2 per group

Units/Longs Spinner, 1 per pair, page 97

Overhead Base Ten Blocks and/or Base Ten Blocks Place-Value Mat transparency (optional)

Overview

In this game for three or four players, children take turns rolling two number cubes to determine the value of the Base Ten Blocks to remove from their place-value mat in an effort to be the first to clear all the blocks off their mat. In this activity, children have the opportunity to:

- ◆ build mental math skills
- ◆ recall basic addition facts
- ◆ trade flats for longs and longs for units.
- ◆ use subtraction

The Activity

Introducing

- ◆ Tell children that they are going to play a game called *Race to Clear the Mat.* Distribute the place-value mats.
- ◆ Go over the game rules given in *On Their Own.*
- ◆ Invite two volunteers to play a demonstration game with you.
- ◆ After you roll the number cubes, point out that you must first trade blocks, 1 long for 10 units, in order to be able to take away the total number of units you rolled.
- ◆ Play for several more turns until children can see that you have to trade the flat for 10 longs and then trade more longs for units.

On Their Own

Play *Race to Clear the Mat!*

Here are the rules.

1. This is a game for 3 or 4 players. The object is to be the first to clear all the Base 10 Blocks off a place-value mat.

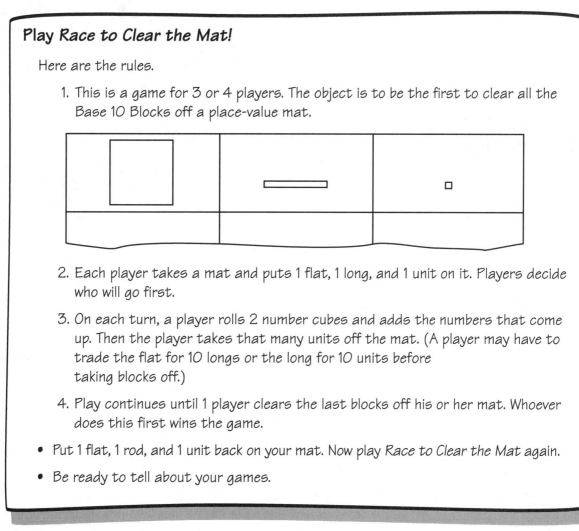

2. Each player takes a mat and puts 1 flat, 1 long, and 1 unit on it. Players decide who will go first.

3. On each turn, a player rolls 2 number cubes and adds the numbers that come up. Then the player takes that many units off the mat. (A player may have to trade the flat for 10 longs or the long for 10 units before taking blocks off.)

4. Play continues until 1 player clears the last blocks off his or her mat. Whoever does this first wins the game.

• Put 1 flat, 1 rod, and 1 unit back on your mat. Now play *Race to Clear the Mat* again.

• Be ready to tell about your games.

The Bigger Picture

Thinking and Sharing

Invite children to talk about their games and describe some of the thinking they did.

Use prompts like these to promote class discussion:

◆ After you rolled the number cubes, how did you find the number of units to clear off your mat?

◆ What was the greatest number you could subtract on a turn? What was the least number you could subtract?

◆ When did you have to trade one kind of block for another kind?

◆ Did you ever have a choice about which blocks to take off your mat? Explain.

◆ Near the end of the game, when you were left with just a few blocks on your mat, were you able to figure out what number you would need to clear your mat? Explain.

Drawing and Writing

Have children describe or draw the blocks on their mat at the beginning of a game. Then have them tell about or draw which blocks they took away and which they had left for several rounds of the game.

Teacher Talk

Where's the Mathematics?

Most children think of *Race to Clear the Mat* as the "opposite" of the game *Race for a Flat.* In fact, they are right! Whereas in *Race for a Flat,* players begin with empty mats and try to fill them with blocks whose value is 100, in *Race to Clear the Mat,* players begin with mats filled with blocks whose value is 111 and they try to empty them.

Race to Clear the Mat requires children to model the process of subtracting one- or two-digit numbers from one-, two-, or three-digit numbers. Children are sometimes asked to regroup, or "trade," from one place-value position to another in order to subtract before they fully understand the concept of subtraction. By experiencing the subtraction operation as they do in this game, children deepen their conceptualization of the meaning of subtraction and why it is sometimes necessary to regroup.

At first, some children may need help in trading and even, perhaps, in removing the number and kinds of blocks that match the sum of the numbers they roll. For example, after rolling a sum of 11, one child may need to trade 1 long for 10 units and put the 10 units into the units column before removing a total of 11 units. Another child will realize that, for a roll of 11, taking 1 long and 1 unit off the mat will do the trick!

Recording subtraction facts throughout the game helps some children to strengthen the connection between the blocks and the numbers they represent. Here is one child's recording of the subtraction facts that took him close to the end of one game. Except for his error in subtracting 7

Extending the Activity

Have children play an alternative version of the game using just one number cube and the *Units/Longs Spinner.* Players roll and spin. They take off their mats the number of blocks rolled—either units or longs, according to the spin. Again, play continues until someone clears all the blocks off a mat.

from 72, the sequence of number sentences tells the complete story of his game, from his start with 111 to the point at which he had 1 unit left. After writing "9 – 8 = 1" this boy announced that he would be the winner after just one more roll. (Of course, he was assuming that his partner wouldn't win on the intervening roll!)

You may wish to have children play a more challenging version of this game in which players clear their mats only by rolling the exact number that remains on the mat. Players may choose to roll just one number cube at any time in this version of the game. (Surely, the player with just 1 more unit to clear off a mat would choose to roll just one number cube!)

$$111 - 11 = 100$$
$$100 - 6 = 94$$
$$94 - 7 = 87$$
$$87 - 10 = 77$$
$$77 - 5 = 72$$
$$72 - 7 = 64$$
$$64 - 9 = 55$$
$$55 - 4 = 51$$
$$51 - 7 = 44$$
$$44 - 7 = 37$$
$$37 - 5 = 32$$
$$32 - 4 = 28$$
$$28 - 10 = 18$$

$$18 - 9 = 9$$
$$9 - 8 = 1$$

SUBTRACTION SPLIT

Getting Ready

What You'll Need

Base Ten Blocks, 1 set per pair

Base Ten Blocks Place-Value Mat, 1 per pair

Base Ten Blocks Cards (1) and *(2)* pages 99–100, 1 deck per pair

Subtraction Split Spinner, 1 per pair, page 101

Trade/No Trade Spinner, 1 per pair, page 98

Overhead Base Ten Blocks (optional)

Overview

In this game for two players, children draw cards to determine whether to use Base Ten Blocks to build a number on a place-value mat or to take blocks that represent a number off the mat. Then children spin a spinner to compare the value of the blocks remaining on the mat to an inequality. In this activity, children have the opportunity to:

♦ subtract two-digit numbers, trading if necessary

♦ compare two-digit numbers

The Activity

Introducing

♦ Distribute *Subtraction Split Spinners,* one to each pair. Help children interpret the meaning of the phrase in each sector.

♦ Call on volunteers to name numbers that are less than 10 and greater than 10, less than 20 and greater than 20, and less than 30 and greater than 30.

♦ Distribute decks of *Base Ten Blocks Cards,* one to a pair. Challenge children to look through their deck and hold up the card that shows blocks that model a given number. Ask them, for example, to hold up the card that shows 25, then 34, and then 43.

♦ Explain the game rules given in *On Their Own.*

♦ Demonstrate by playing a partial game of *Subtraction Split* with a volunteer.

On Their Own

Play *Subtraction Split!*

Here are the rules.

1. This is a game for 2 players. The object is to have more cards than the other player has at the end of the game.

2. Players each draw a *Base 10 Blocks Card*.
   - Whoever gets the card that shows the *greater* number uses blocks to build that number on a place-value mat.
   - Then, whoever gets the card that shows the *lesser* number takes blocks for that number off the mat.

3. Players name the number shown by the blocks left on the mat.

4. One player spins a spinner that looks like this.

5. What does the spinner land on? Do the blocks left on the mat fit this?

   - If so, then whoever spun gets both cards.
   - If not, then whoever did not spin gets both cards.

6. Again, players draw cards. They build and take away blocks. They take turns spinning.

7. When there are no more cards left to draw, the player with more cards wins.

- Play *Subtraction Split* again.

- Be ready to talk about your games.

The Bigger Picture

Thinking and Sharing

Invite children to talk about their games and describe some of the thinking they did.

Use prompts like these to promote class discussion:

- How did you decide whether you had to build your number on the mat or take blocks for your number off the mat?

- When did you have to trade in order to take blocks away?

- How did you know if the number left on the mat was greater than 10 or less than 10? if it was greater than 20 or less than 20? if it was greater than 30 or less than 30?

- Could you use a strategy to help you win this game? Explain.

Writing and Drawing

Have children describe the cards they held that modeled the greatest and least numbers at the end of the last game. Then have them illustrate their work by drawing the blocks that appear on each card.

Teacher Talk

Where's the Mathematics?

Subtraction Split is itself "split" into two parts. For the first part of the game, children draw cards in tandem. Together they compare the block configurations shown on their cards. If they have difficulty determining which configuration shows the greater number and which shows the lesser, be sure to intervene and direct them use Base Ten Blocks to build both configurations *off* the mat. Being able to "see" the numbers modeled with blocks should help children compare them correctly. The player who drew the card that shows the greater number can slide the block configuration onto the place-value mat. The player who drew the lesser number can then take away blocks that represent that number from the blocks on the mat.

The second part of the game requires further cooperation that involves critical thinking. Together players identify the number represented by the blocks that remain on their mat after subtracting (the difference in the subtraction problem). They spin the *Subtraction Split Spinner* and then, depending on where the spinner lands, they compare their difference to the numbers 10, 20, or 30. Some children may decide that their difference is greater than a particular multiple of ten, but not understand that it is at the same time also less than other numbers. Other children may need to use blocks to build the multiple of ten indicated on each sector of the spinner in order to compare it with their difference.

The following exercise can be useful in helping children to identify their difference as being greater or less than the three multiples of ten. Copy this

Extending the Activity

Have children play the game again, this time using the *Trade/No Trade Spinner* instead of the *Subtraction Split Spinner.* If a spin of this spinner lands on *Trade,* then each player who must trade in order to subtract gets a point. If the spinner lands on *No Trade,* then each player who does not have to trade gets a point. The player with more points at the end of this game wins.

---

chart on the board. Then, ask volunteers to suggest some numbers that belong in each row. Record their responses on the chart.

Numbers that are:

greater than 10 ——→	
less than 10 ——→	
greater than 20 ——→	
less than 20 ——→	
greater than 30 ——→	
less than 30 ——→	

Asking children to suggest other ways for finding whether the number left on their mat was greater or less than 10, 20, or 30 channels them to focus on the process of subtraction, rather than on the answer to the subtraction problem.

Because children must work closely together at each stage of this game, they may not realize that this is a game of chance, not a game of strategy. After playing several games of *Subtraction Split* they should begin to understand that this is true because the game is based on drawing cards at random and on the random spins of the spinner.

SUM IT UP!

Getting Ready

What You'll Need

Base Ten Blocks, 1 set per group

Sum It Up! worksheet, 1 or 2 per group, page 102

Overhead Base Ten Blocks and/or *Sum It Up!* worksheet transparency (optional)

Overview

Children use Base Ten Blocks to model a number as the sum of two addends. Then they find ways to model the same number with different pairs of addends. In this activity, children have the opportunity to:

◆ reinforce number recognition

◆ use counting and addition skills

◆ record the sum of two 2-digit numbers

The Activity

Make sure that children know the meanings of the terms addend *and* sum. *Explain that the answer to an addition example is called the sum and that a sum is the number that results from adding two or more addends at once.*

Introducing

◆ Display 1 long and 8 units and have children do the same.

◆ Count the blocks aloud with the class to establish that they model the number 18.

◆ Invite a volunteer to separate the blocks into two groups and name the value of each, saying, for example, "This group has 12 and that group has 6."

◆ Now ask the volunteer to push the two groups together. Record an addition sentence for this action on the chalkboard; for example, 12 + 6 = 18.

◆ Invite another volunteer to use 18 units to make and identify two different groups.

◆ Ask another volunteer to push these two groups together and record an addition sentence for this action; for example, 9 + 9 = 18. Elicit that the addition sentences on the board have the same sum, even though they have different addends.

◆ Push all the blocks together again. Invite other children to each make two different groups from the 18 and then put their groups together and write an addition sentence to record what they did.

◆ Reiterate that all children's addition sentences have the same sum, 18.

On Their Own

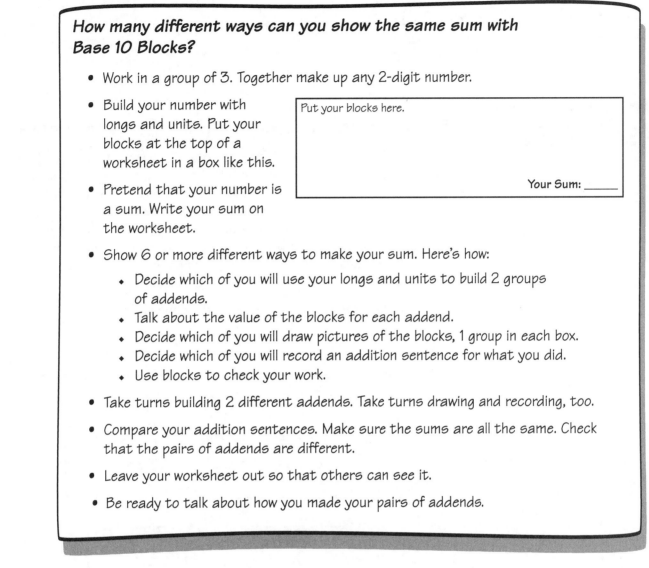

How many different ways can you show the same sum with Base 10 Blocks?

- Work in a group of 3. Together make up any 2-digit number.

- Build your number with longs and units. Put your blocks at the top of a worksheet in a box like this.

  Put your blocks here.

  Your Sum: _____

- Pretend that your number is a sum. Write your sum on the worksheet.

- Show 6 or more different ways to make your sum. Here's how:
  - Decide which of you will use your longs and units to build 2 groups of addends.
  - Talk about the value of the blocks for each addend.
  - Decide which of you will draw pictures of the blocks, 1 group in each box.
  - Decide which of you will record an addition sentence for what you did.
  - Use blocks to check your work.

- Take turns building 2 different addends. Take turns drawing and recording, too.

- Compare your addition sentences. Make sure the sums are all the same. Check that the pairs of addends are different.

- Leave your worksheet out so that others can see it.

- Be ready to talk about how you made your pairs of addends.

The Bigger Picture

Thinking and Sharing

Invite groups to exchange worksheets and then discuss among themselves how the other groups built the addends for their sum.

Use prompts like these to promote class discussion:

- How were your number sentences alike? How were they different?

- Did your group find all the possible ways to show your sum? How do you know?

- When it was your turn to build two addends for the sum, what did you think about first?

- Which job did you like better, building two addends for your sum, drawing the blocks for someone else's addends, or writing the addition sentence? Why?

Writing

Tell children to "sum up" how they decided on a particular pair of addends to build to show their group's sum.

Where's the Mathematics?

Cooperative learning is the key to successfully completing the *Sum It Up!* activity. Agreeing on a number to model will be each threesome's first hurdle. Agreeing on who will do what for each combination of addends will be their second. The value of having children work in this way is that each of them gets an opportunity to build different pairs of addends and then draw and record them on their group's worksheet, thus contributing to the production of a single document. (Groups that find more than six pairs of addends for their sums can use another worksheet.)

The worksheet shown here was produced by one group that "made up" the number 23.

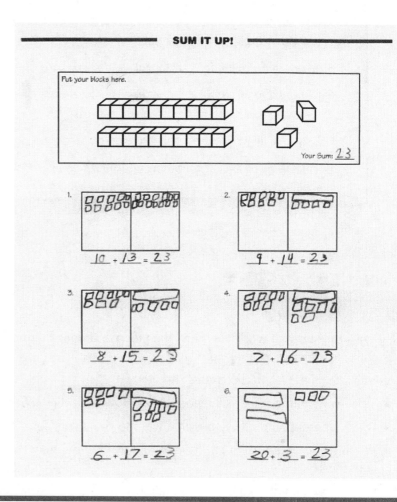

Extending the Activity

Have children repeat the activity, but this time challenge them to make *three* addends for their group's original sum. (Alternatively, you might suggest that any group whose first sum was small can now choose a sum greater than the first.)

As children try to find all possible pairs of addends for a sum, many of them will decide to start with a particular addend pair and then find another pair by raising one addend by a particular amount and then lowering the other by the same amount, thus being sure to maintain the constant sum. This was the clearly the reasoning of the child who wrote the following. He explains in his last sentence: "Next, I lowered the first number and highered the second."

I did 10 + 10 = 20 and 20 + 3 = 23 so I did 10 + 13 = 23. nekst I lord the frst nudr and hird the sekint.

"Twenty-three" remained a favorite of this child who went on to record trios of *three* addends for this sum.

$$9 + 4 + 10 = 23$$

$$8 + 10 + 5 = 23$$

$$10 + 10 + 3 = 23$$
$$7 + 10 + 6 = 23$$
$$6 + 10 + 7 = 23$$
$$20 + 2 + 1 = 23$$

WAY TO PAY

Getting Ready

What You'll Need

Base Ten Blocks, 1 set per pair

What Will You Buy? worksheet, 1 per pair, page 103

Base Ten Blocks Place-Value mat, 1 per child

Overhead Base Ten Blocks (optional)

Overview

Using Base Ten units, longs, and flats to represent pennies, dimes, and dollars respectively, children find two or more block combinations with which to pay for something they want to buy. In this activity, children have the opportunity to:

◆ model three-digit numbers

◆ build addition skills

◆ internalize the relationship between pennies, dimes, and dollars

The Activity

Introducing

◆ Model a three-digit number on a place-value mat using longs and units only. For example, display fourteen longs and five units.

◆ Call on a volunteer to identify the number.

◆ Ask children to model the number 145 on their own mats in a different way.

◆ For this example, children are likely to display one flat, four longs, and five units. Elicit that by displaying the number (145) in this way they used fewer blocks than you did.

◆ Write the number on the chalkboard. Then insert a dollar sign and a decimal point.

◆ Point to the amount on the board and tell children to pretend that units are pennies. Elicit that (145) pennies have the same value as this amount, ($1.45).

On Their Own

How can you show a way to pay for something with Base 10 Blocks?

- Work with a partner. Pretend that the blocks are different kinds of money. Here's what block money is worth:

  1 unit = 1 penny, or 1¢

  1 long = 1 dime, or 10¢

  1 flat = 1 dollar, 100¢, or $1.00

- Look at a worksheet like this to see all the things you can buy. Together decide on something to buy.

- Put blocks on a place-value mat to show a way to pay for what you buy.

- Your partner should put blocks on another place-value mat to show a different way to pay for the same things.

- Are there other ways to pay for this with blocks? Record all the ways.

- Now decide on something else to buy. Take turns being first to show a way to pay.

- Be ready to talk about your ways to pay.

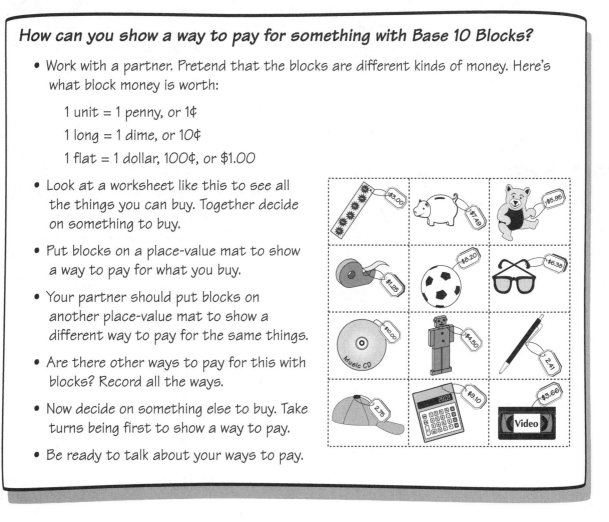

The Bigger Picture

Thinking and Sharing

Cut apart a *What Will You Buy?* worksheet. Stand up the twelve pictured items across the chalkboard ledge. (You may want to first enlarge the worksheet on a copier to make the items and their price tags more visible from a distance.) Alternatively, write the names of the items with their prices across the board. Then have pairs of children post their "ways to pay" for each item below it.

Use prompts like these to promote class discussion:

- How many ways did you find to pay for _____? Tell about each way.

- What is another way to pay for _____? Explain.

- Which way to pay for _____ used the least number of blocks? Which way used the greatest number of blocks?

- What are some reasons for paying for something with the least number of dollars and coins possible?

- Why might someone want to pay with a greater number of dollars and coins than necessary?

Writing

Bring supermarket sale flyers or newspaper ads to class. Allow children to pick out a sale item that they would like to buy. Tell them to imagine that they could pay for that item with Base Ten Blocks. Have them describe how they would pay for the item with the least number of blocks.

Teacher Talk

Where's the Mathematics?

To help reinforce the notion of Base Ten Blocks having equivalent monetary values, distribute play money (dollar bills, dimes, and pennies), one of each to a child. Have children put the money at the top of their place-value mats—a dollar on the flat, a dime on the long, and a penny on the unit—to serve as constant reminders of the equivalencies.

Of course, there is no Base Ten Block representation of a nickel. Eager to extend the activity by using nickels, however, some classes have made Base Ten "nickels" by lining up groups of five units, end to end, on pieces of tape. They sometimes rule another column on their place-value mats—between the units and longs columns—and place their Base Ten nickel at the top. Some children have gone even further by using rubber bands to hold two longs and a strip of five units together to create Base Ten "quarters"!

Extending the Activity

Alter the prices on a *What Will You Buy?* worksheet by moving the decimal point on each price tag one place to the right. (For example, the strip of stickers would "cost" $30.00, the piggy bank would cost $74.90, and so on.) Copy and distribute these worksheets. Then tell children to pretend that all the blocks are now worth dollars—with 1 unit equal to $1, 1 long equal to $10, and 1 flat equal to $100. Have children do the activity again using these greater block values.

Most children can grasp the notion that "paying" for something with the *least number* of blocks is the most efficient way to pay. They may explain this by saying that paying with the least number of dollars and coins saves time ("It's faster to count out less money than more money") and takes up less space in a store's cash register ("A dime takes up less space than 10 pennies").

It may be more difficult for some children to imagine why someone might want to pay with a *greater number* of dollars and coins than necessary. Again, the answer is for efficiency's sake. People might want to lessen the number of coins that they themselves are carrying ("Ten pennies would make your pocket heavier than one dime"). One child appeared incredulous when she realized that the way to pay for anything with the greatest number of coins possible is by using only pennies. (The notion of carrying 1,000 pennies to the store to pay for the $10 Music CD kept her laughing throughout the day!)

Having children examine advertisements and allowing them to pick out actual items that they might want to buy models real-world experiences. After mulling over a supermarker flyer, the child whose work follows decided that she would "buy" corn chips sale priced at $1.59.

> I would by chips for $1.59 I would use
> 1 flat 5 longs 9 units that would be the
> lest number to by the chips

WHAT PRICE LUNCH?

Getting Ready

What You'll Need

Base Ten Blocks, 1 set per pair

Base Ten Blocks Place-Value Mat, 1 per pair

1–100 Grid, 1 per pair, page 95

Lunch Money Cards, 1 set (glued onto a backing and cut apart) per pair, page 104

Base Ten Block Grid Paper, several sheets per pair, page 109

Overview

Children use Base Ten Blocks to model an amount of money. Then they pick cards that indicate other amounts, which they model with blocks, in an effort to collect enough blocks to represent $5. In this activity, children have the opportunity to:

- work with money concepts

- compare and combine numerical quantities

- apply strategies for adding amounts of money

The Activity

Introducing

- Display one unit and tell children to pretend that the unit is a penny (worth 1¢).

- Display one long and one flat. Elicit that since a unit is a penny, then a long is a dime (worth 10¢) and a flat is a dollar (worth 100¢, or $1.00).

- Draw the following amounts on the chalkboard.

  $$35¢ \quad 96¢ \quad 7¢$$

- Divide the class into three groups. Have each group use Base Ten Blocks to build one of the amounts on a place-value mat.

- Tell children to pretend that they want to buy something that costs *ten cents more* than they have on their mat. Have them add blocks to their mat to show the ten cents. Call on a volunteer from each group to announce the new amount.

- Now tell children to pretend that they want to buy something that costs *one dollar more* than they have on their mat. Have them add blocks to their mat to show the dollar. Ask volunteers to name the new amounts.

On Their Own

How can you use Base 10 Blocks to "buy lunch"?

- Work with a partner. Toss a unit onto a 1–100 Grid. Pretend that the unit lands on an amount of money.

- Get blocks to show this amount. Put the blocks on a place-value mat. Record the amount.
    - Pretend you need money to buy lunch—for you *and* your partner.
    - But, lunch for 2 costs $5.00!

- Use cards like these to help you get more lunch money.

Turn the 6 cards face down. Mix them.

- Pick 1 card. Take blocks to match the blocks on your card. Put them on your mat. (Remember: 1 long = 10¢ and 1 flat = $1.00.) How much money do you have now? Record the amount.

- Pick another card. Add blocks that match the ones on this card to your mat. Record. Do you have $5.00 yet? If not, pick again.

- When you get at least $5.00, say "Lunch time"!

- Still hungry? Repeat the activity to get enough money for tomorrow's lunch!

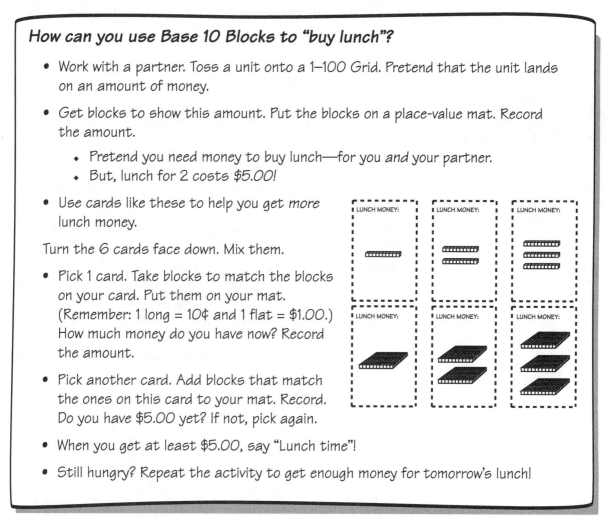

The Bigger Picture

Thinking and Sharing

Invite pairs to write their starting amounts on the board, tell how much money they added with each pick, and write the amount of money they collected for "lunch."

Use prompts like these to promote class discussion:

- How did your starting amount change if your first pick was 10¢ (20¢/30¢)? How would the same starting amount have changed if your first pick was $1 ($2/$3)?

- How many picks did you need to get to $5? What were your picks?

- Did you get exactly $5? If not, how much more than $5 did you get?

- Did you ever have to trade blocks? Explain.

- Did you add any of the new amounts in your head? If so, tell how you did this.

Writing

Have children describe how they knew whether they had reached $5 or whether they had to pick again to get to $5.

Where's the Mathematics?

As children pick *Lunch Money Cards* and record the amounts that appear on the cards they pick, they gain practice not only in adding multiples of ten (10, 20, 30) and multiples of a hundred (100, 200, 300) but also in keeping a running total.

Pairs should be able to accumulate enough money to "buy their lunch" with just a few picks. The recording below shows the work of one pair that collected lunch money for three days. In each case, their final pick brought them over the required minimum of $5. (They quickly dubbed the amounts over $5 as "snack money"!) For the first day, the pair's first four picks brought them a total of $3.94. Then they picked the $2 *Lunch Money Card,* which gave them a grand total of $5.94. For the second day, four picks got the pair enough money for lunch. For the third day, just two picks got them enough for lunch.

1. $14¢ + 20¢ = 34¢ + 30¢ = 64¢ + 30¢ = 1¢$
   $+ \$3.00 = \$3.94 + \$2.00 = \$5.94.$

2. $96¢ + \$3.00 = \$3.98 + 10¢ = \$4.08 + 20¢$
   $= \$4.28 + \$1.00 = \$5.28$

3. $25¢ + \$3.00 = \$3.25 + \$2.00 = \$5.25$

Extending the Activity

Bring a restaurant menu to class. Allow children to each pretend to order two or three items from the menu. Have them model their amounts on a place-value mat and tell the total amount that they would need to buy their meal.

Some pairs will have to trade blocks as they work. If children happen to pick a long sequence of cards that shows only multiples of ten, they may collect so many longs that they have to trade ten of them for a flat.

Giving children a chance to choose what to order from a restaurant menu motivates them towards decision making. At the same time, children gain informal addition experience, some of which may depend on skills that they do not already have. For example, the child who chose to illustrate his "lunch" of pizza, a slushy, a vanilla cone, and a banana had to find the sum of the four items, priced at $1.60, 9¢, 50¢, and 43¢ respectively. Although this child had not yet learned how to regroup for addition, by working with the Base Ten Blocks and trading longs for flats, he found the total, $2.62.

WHAT'S THE DIFFERENCE?

Getting Ready

What You'll Need

Base Ten Blocks, 1 set per pair

What's the Difference? Gameboard, 1 per pair, page 106

Counters of two different colors, 1 of each color per pair

One-or-Two Spinner, 1 per pair, page 105

Index cards

Overhead Base Ten Blocks and/or *What's the Difference?* Gameboard transparency (optional)

The Activity

Overview

In this game for two players, children use Base Ten Blocks to find given differences as they move around a gameboard in an effort to be the first to get to the finish line. In this activity, children have the opportunity to:

- ◆ explore the meaning of subtraction
- ◆ record basic subtraction facts

Introducing

- ◆ Ask children to tell what the answer to an addition example is called.
- ◆ Explain that just as "sum" is the word for the answer to an addition example, there is a word for the answer to a subtraction example.
- ◆ Elicit that the word for the answer to a subtraction example is "difference."
- ◆ Ask someone to name a number between zero and ten. Model the suggested number with units.
- ◆ Write an open subtraction sentence on the chalkboard (either horizontally or vertically) with the suggested number as the difference. For example, if a child named 7, you would write __ – __ = 7.
- ◆ Call for a pair of numbers for which 7 could be the difference.
- ◆ Have a volunteer put two more groups of units with the model to show how one group of units take away the other group of units results in the difference, in this case, 7. After checking the child's work allow him or her to record it by completing the open subtraction sentence.
- ◆ Call on other volunteers to model and record subtraction sentences that have the same difference.

On Their Own

Play What's the Difference?

Here are the rules.

1. Get counters so you and your partner can move from START to FINISH on a gameboard that looks like this.

2. Take turns spinning the 1-or-2 Spinner.

3. Spin! Move 1 or 2 spaces to match your spin.

4. The number you land on is the *difference* for a subtraction fact. Use units to find a subtraction fact that has this difference.

5. Record your subtraction fact on a card. Have your partner check your work.

6. Continue playing until someone gets to the 5 at the FINISH line.

7. Play 2 more games of *What's the Difference?*

8. Be ready to talk about the subtraction facts you found.

Start					
3	5	1	8	0	2
					7
					4
4	7	2	3	6	1
0					
5					
8					Finish
1	6	2	9	5	

The Bigger Picture

Thinking and Sharing

Invite children to talk about their games and describe some of the thinking they did.

Use prompts like these to promote class discussion:

- What was hard about this activity? What was easy?

- How did you go about finding a subtraction fact for a difference?

- Did you ever think of more than one fact for a difference? If so, what was the difference? What facts did you think of? How did you decide which fact to use?

- Did you show and write the same fact more than once? Was there any other fact that you could have written?

Extending the Activity

1. You may wish to have children play a simpler version of this game. Tell children that the number they land on is the difference that remains when they subtract a mystery number from 10. Record an open subtraction sentence for this as: 10 − (mystery number) = (landing number). As children play, have them first record each number they land on as the

Where's the Mathematics?

The title of this activity, *What's the Difference?,* is a play on words that may elude some children. Make sure that children understand that the word "difference" has a special meaning in math. Point out that the answer to a subtraction problem is called the *difference.*

As children move their counters around the game board in response to the spin of a spinner, they may land on the same "difference" more than once. When this happens, children start to realize that there are many possible minuend-and-subtrahend combinations that share the same difference.

$$8 - 6 = 2$$

$$7 - 5 = 2$$

$$10 - 8 = 2$$

One child who landed on all three game board spaces marked "2" wrote these number sentences. The second time this child landed on 2, he thought that he would rewrite the first sentence he wrote for the difference 2. As he began to write, however, another subtraction sentence came to mind and so he recorded it instead. When he landed on 2 a third time, the child no longer considered rewriting either of his first two sentences and eagerly wrote yet another subtraction sentence for the same difference.

difference for the open sentence and then complete the sentence by finding the mystery number.

2. Challenge children to play the game again, this time using both longs and units and finding two 2-digit subtraction examples for each difference they land on.

When children record their subtraction sentences for their unit models, they learn to make the connection between the concrete and the abstract. Children also come to realize the importance of recording numbers in the correct order to show subtraction. A child who writes 3 – 10 instead of 10 – 3 for the difference 7 and is corrected by a partner will then realize that the order in which the numbers are recorded is important.

This game helps children to develop an intuitive understanding of "taking away" even before they learn the traditional subtraction algorithm. When children experience subtraction in this concrete way, building number models and then recording the numbers they represent, they internalize the process.

WHAT'S THE DIFFERENCE? GAMEBOARD

Start

3	5	1	8	0	2
					7
					4

4	7	2	3	6	1
0					
5					
8					Finish
1	6	2	9	5	

WHO'S GOT THE MOST?

- Addition
- Place value
- Number relationships

Getting Ready

What You'll Need

Base Ten Blocks, 1 set per group

Base Ten Blocks Cards (1) and *(2)* pages 99–100, 1 deck per group

Base Ten Blocks Place-Value Mat, 1 per child

Units/Longs Spinner, 1 per pair, page 97

Trade/No Trade Spinner, 1 per pair, page 98

Units/Longs/Flats Spinner, 1 per pair, page 107

Overhead Base Ten Blocks (optional)

Overview

In this game for two to five players, children use Base Ten Blocks to model two 2-digit numbers. They collect points depending on whether the sum of their numbers represents the greatest number of longs or the greatest number of units. In this activity, children have the opportunity to:

- ◆ add two-digit numbers and trade if necessary
- ◆ use place value to add longs and units

The Activity

Introducing

- ◆ Choose any two of the *Base Ten Blocks Cards.* Draw the formation of longs and units that appears on each on the chalkboard.
- ◆ Call on volunteers to come to the board to write the number that each formation represents below it.
- ◆ Have children use blocks to copy each formation.
- ◆ Challenge children to use their blocks to find the sum, the total value of the blocks modeled by both formations.
- ◆ Explain the game rules given in *On Their Own.*
- ◆ Demonstrate *Who Has the Most?* by playing a partial game either alone or with a volunteer.

On Their Own

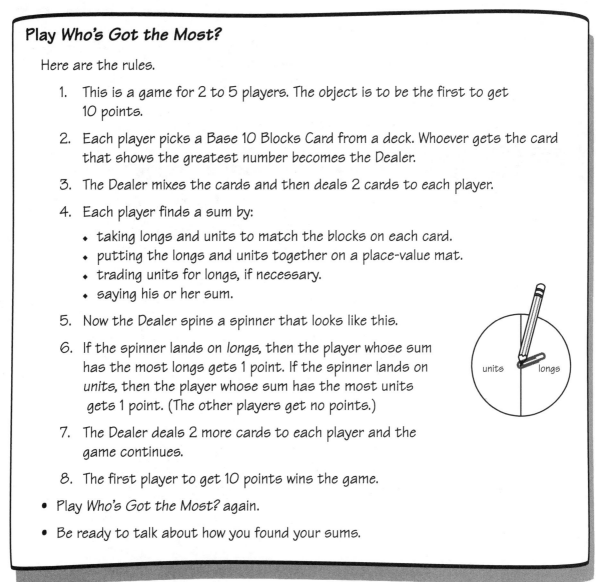

Play *Who's Got the Most?*

Here are the rules.

1. This is a game for 2 to 5 players. The object is to be the first to get 10 points.

2. Each player picks a Base 10 Blocks Card from a deck. Whoever gets the card that shows the greatest number becomes the Dealer.

3. The Dealer mixes the cards and then deals 2 cards to each player.

4. Each player finds a sum by:
   - taking longs and units to match the blocks on each card.
   - putting the longs and units together on a place-value mat.
   - trading units for longs, if necessary.
   - saying his or her sum.

5. Now the Dealer spins a spinner that looks like this.

6. If the spinner lands on *longs*, then the player whose sum has the most longs gets 1 point. If the spinner lands on *units*, then the player whose sum has the most units gets 1 point. (The other players get no points.)

7. The Dealer deals 2 more cards to each player and the game continues.

8. The first player to get 10 points wins the game.

- Play *Who's Got the Most?* again.
- Be ready to talk about how you found your sums.

The Bigger Picture

Thinking and Sharing

Invite children to talk about their games and describe some of the thinking they did.

Use prompts like these to promote class discussion:

- Was using the place-value mat helpful in finding your sum? Explain.
- After you found your sum, how did you know if you had to trade?
- Did more than one player ever have "the most" longs or "the most" units at the same time? If so, what happened then?
- Was it easier to find some sums than others? Explain.
- Were you able to use a strategy to help you win this game? Explain.

Extending the Activity

1. Have children play the game again, this time using the *Trade/No Trade Spinner* instead of the *Units/Longs Spinner*. If this spinner lands on *Trade,* then each player who must trade in order to find a sum gets a point. If the spinner lands on *No Trade,* then each player who does not have to trade gets a point. The player who has the most points when the cards run out is the winner.

Teacher Talk

Where's the Mathematics?

Who Has the Most? is a game that heightens children's number sense. As they build block configurations that match those pictured on cards, children informally compare numbers by comparing the numbers of longs and units that represent them.

In order to add some two 2-digit numbers, a child may need to trade units for longs. A child who lacks the knowledge of why and how to regroup may announce that a number that requires trading is part of the sum in its entirety. For example, one child who held the cards for 38 and 46 first modeled these numbers on his place-value mat. He then looked at the blocks in the longs and units column, added the blocks within each column, and announced that the sum was "seventy fourteen"!

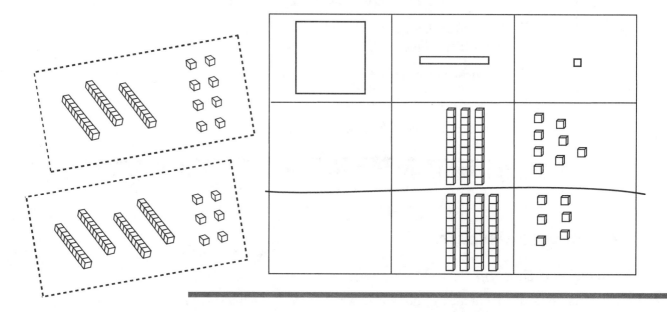

2. Challenge children to play the game by having them work with three-digit numbers. Have them start the game by adding one flat (100) to the number they represent for each card. Then each player should model two 3-digit numbers and find their sum. The Dealer spins a *Units/Longs/Flats Spinner.* A point goes to whoever has the greatest number of the kind of block on which the spinner lands.

Generally, only one player can get a point for each round of this game. Of course, if more than one player has either the most longs or the most units (depending on where the spinner lands), then others can score on the round as well. (To avoid children's becoming frustrated at potentially playing for several rounds without scoring, you may wish to limit the number of players in each group to two or three.)

As children build their pair of number models for their cards and then find the sum of the values, they are informally working with the commutative property of addition. By adding the blocks on her mat, one girl discovered that the sum of her two numbers, 12 and 23, was the same regardless of the order in which she added.

> "I added two and three and got five. Then I added the longs—ten and twenty—and got thirty. So, that's thirty-five. But then I decided to add the blocks the other way.
>
> I added the three and the two and I got five again. When I added the longs this time, I added the two longs to the one to get three longs, or thirty. So now I got thirty-five again. See, it didn't matter if I added upwards or downwards, I still got the same sum!"

When children are able to explain whether "...it was easier to find some sums than others," they demonstrate that they are analyzing the addition process and not merely answering the addition problem. Having students share their ideas about combining numbers helps them to clarify their own understanding, thus strengthening their mental-math abilities.

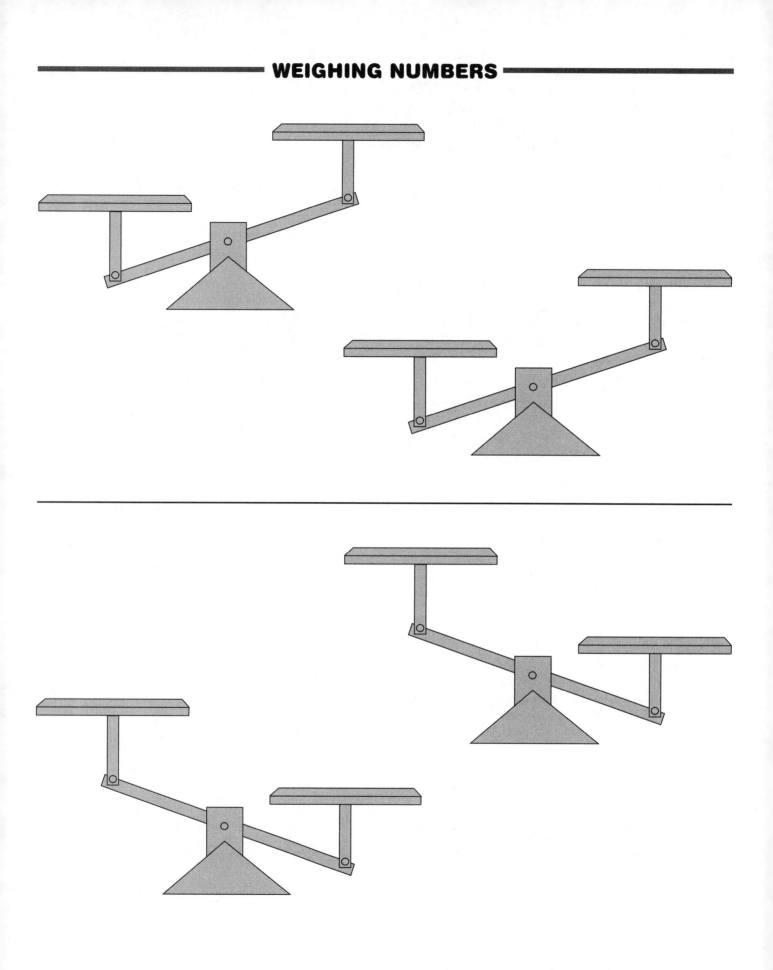

50	25	11
18	38	40
46	29	21

16	28	30
37	13	48
19	42	26

26	44	31
22	12	36
50	49	16

47	39	19
20	17	44
15	35	33

64	52	79
71	80	53
92	67	84

76	71	85
63	90	54
56	62	94

55	90	73
88	58	97
64	69	82

86	65	51
53	94	83
61	68	70

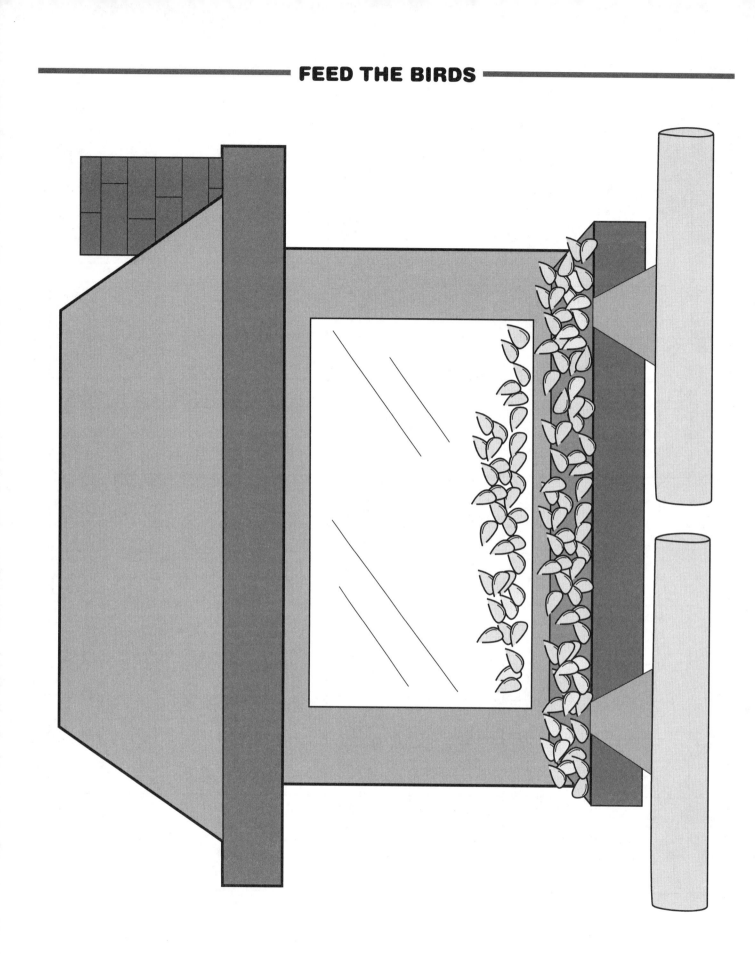

1	2	3	4	5	6	7	8	9	10
11	12	13	14	15	16	17	18	19	20
21	22	23	24	25	26	27	28	29	30
31	32	33	34	35	36	37	38	39	40
41	42	43	44	45	46	47	48	49	50
51	52	53	54	55	56	57	58	59	60
61	62	63	64	65	66	67	68	69	70
71	72	73	74	75	76	77	78	79	80
81	82	83	84	85	86	87	88	89	90
91	92	93	94	95	96	97	98	99	100

LOOKING FOR LENGTH

Put your first object here:

Estimate the length.
Our estimate: _____ units long

Measure the length.
Actual measurement: _____ units long

- -

Put your second object here:

Estimate the length.
Our estimate: _____ units long

Measure the length.
Actual measurement: _____ units long

- -

Put your third object here:

Estimate the length.
Our estimate: _____ units long

Measure the length.
Actual measurement: _____ units long

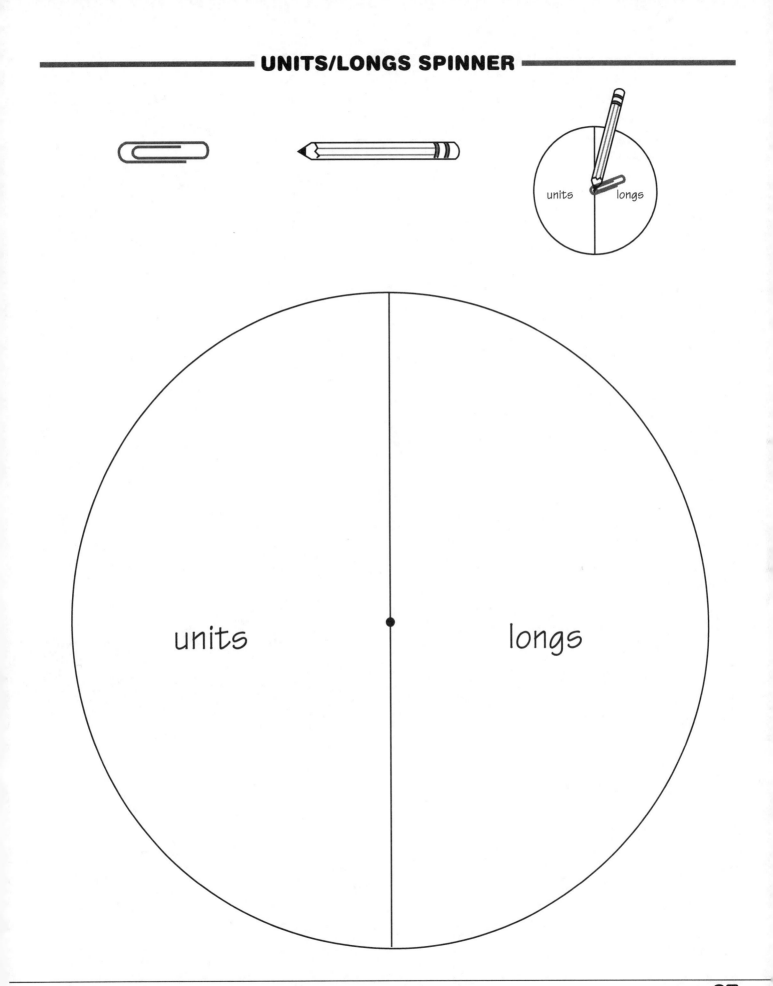

units

longs

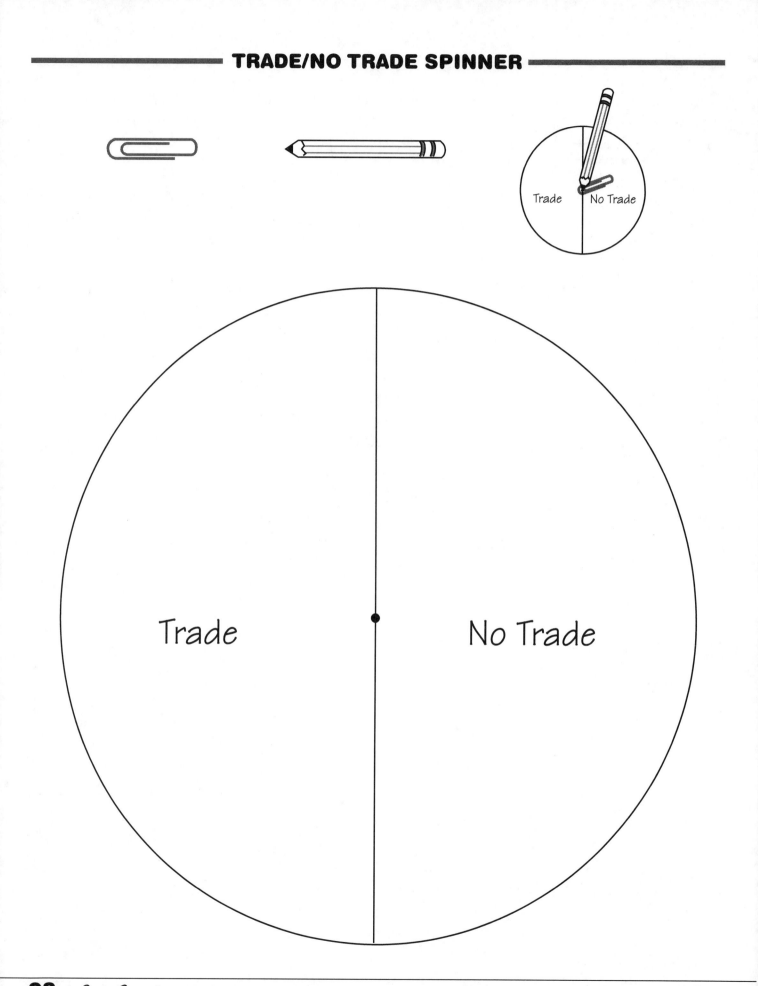

BASE TEN BLOCKS CARDS (1)

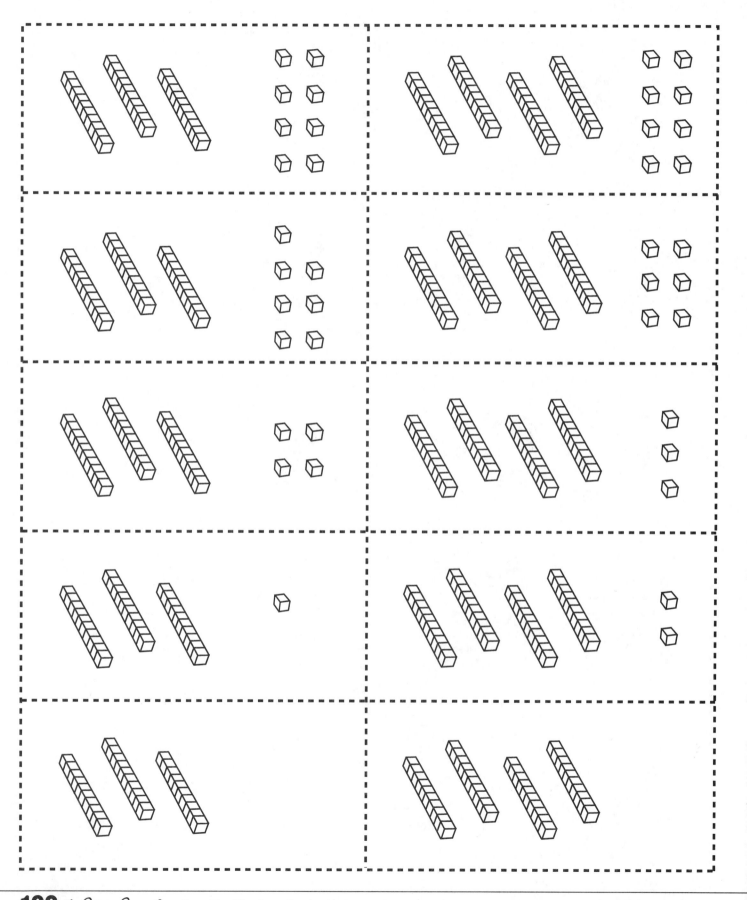

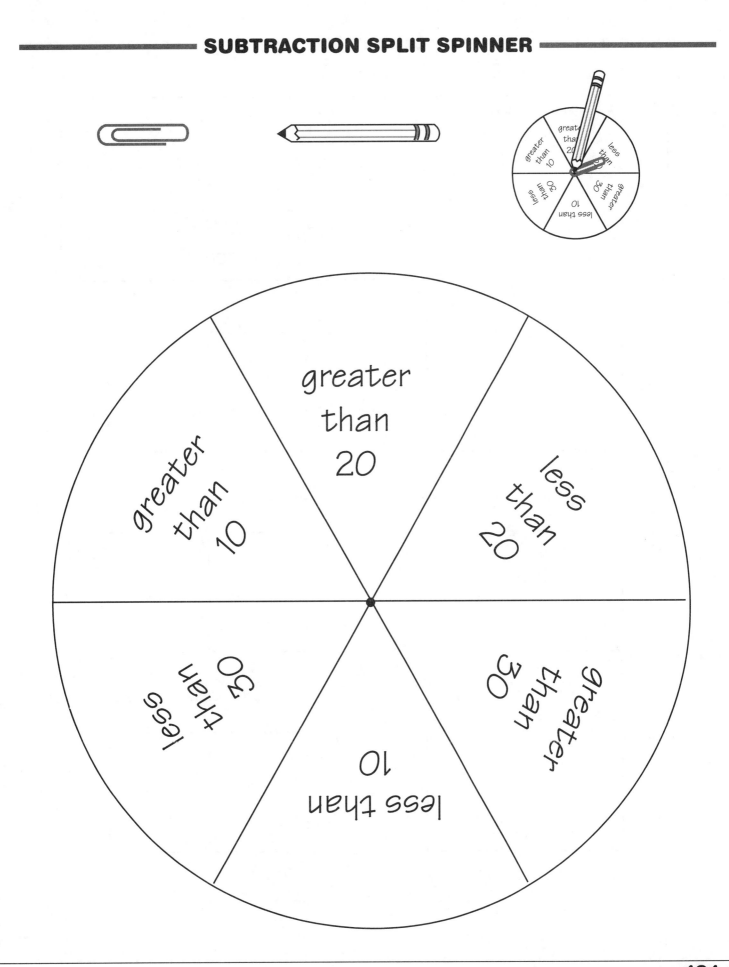

Put your blocks here.

Your Sum: _____

1. _____ + _____ = _____

2. _____ + _____ = _____

3. _____ + _____ = _____

4. _____ + _____ = _____

5. _____ + _____ = _____

6. _____ + _____ = _____

WHAT WILL YOU BUY?

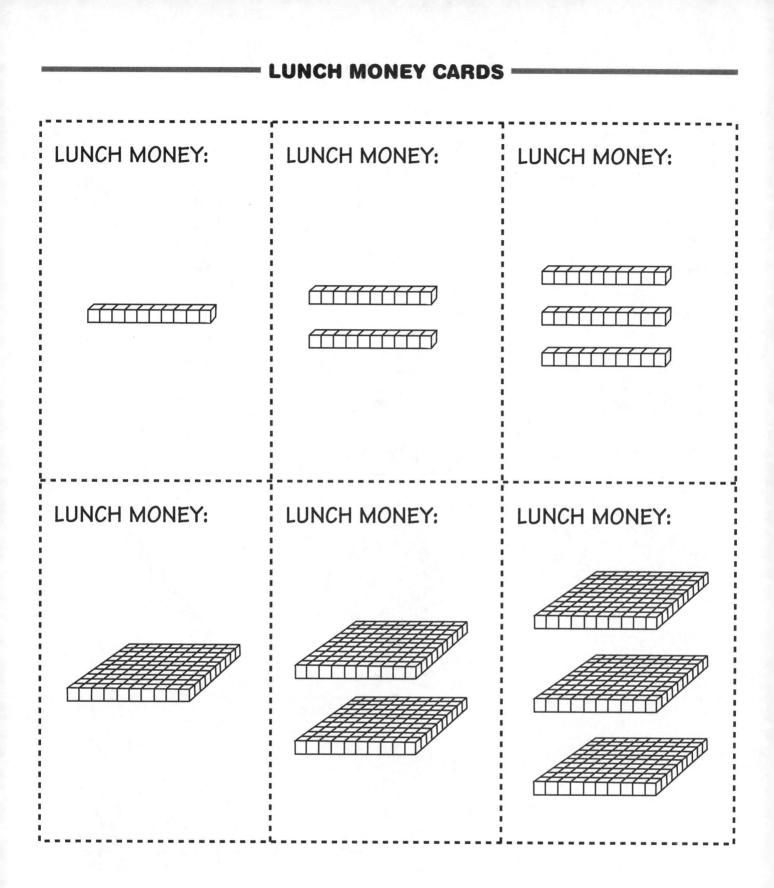

LUNCH MONEY:

LUNCH MONEY:

LUNCH MONEY:

LUNCH MONEY:

LUNCH MONEY:

LUNCH MONEY:

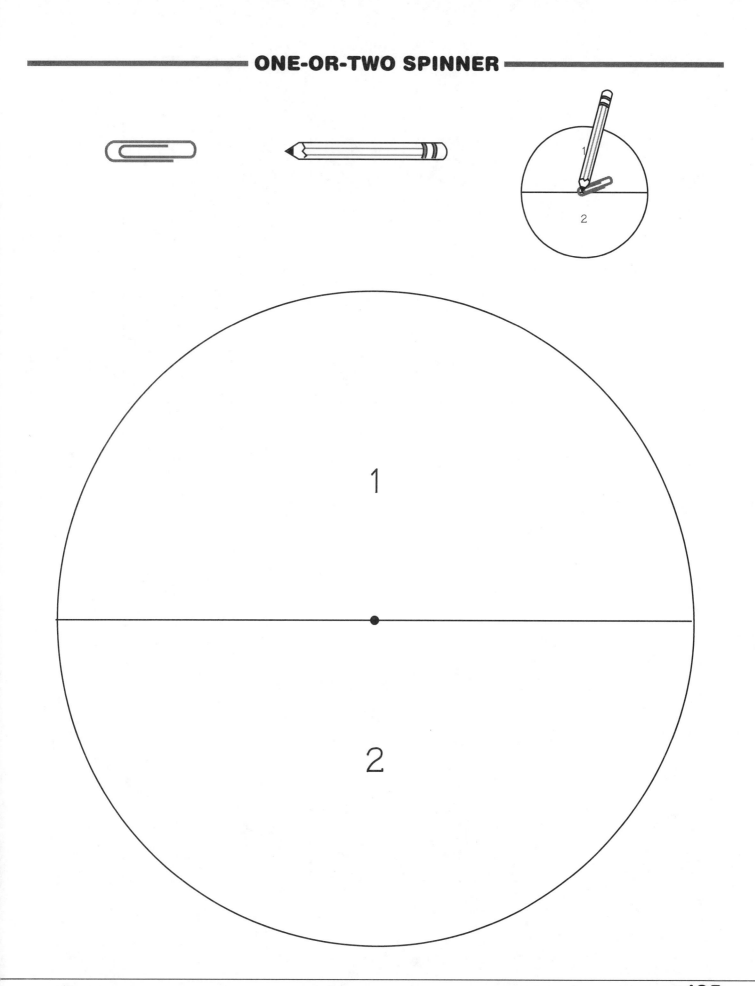

WHAT'S THE DIFFERENCE? GAMEBOARD

Start

3	5	1	8	0	2

7

4

4	7	2	3	6	1

0

5

8

Finish

1	6	2	9	5

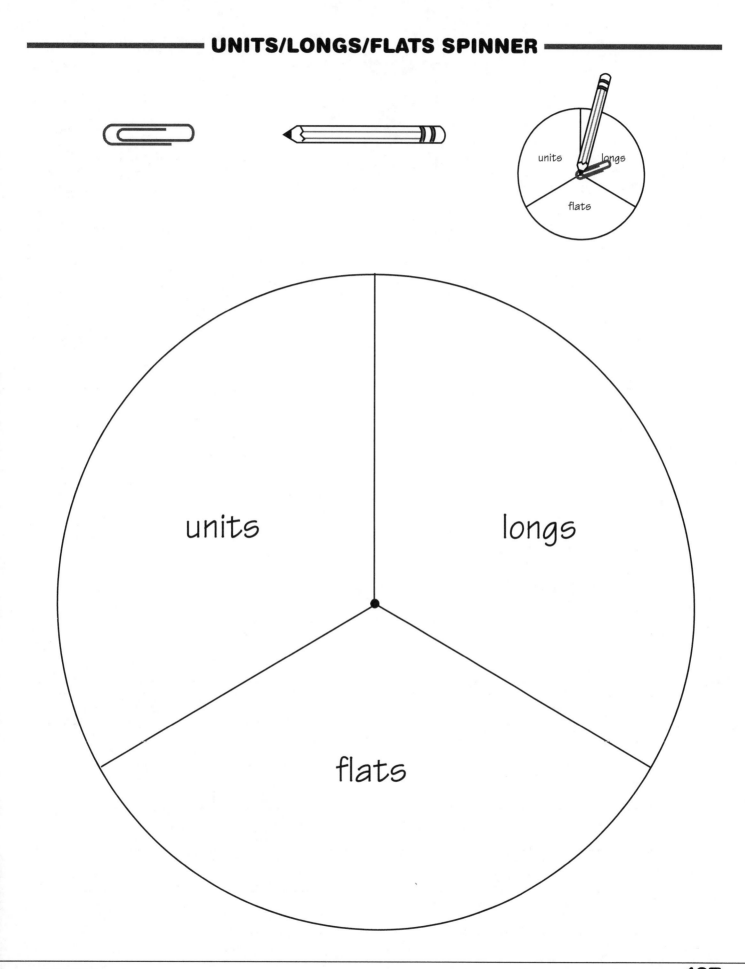

units

longs

flats

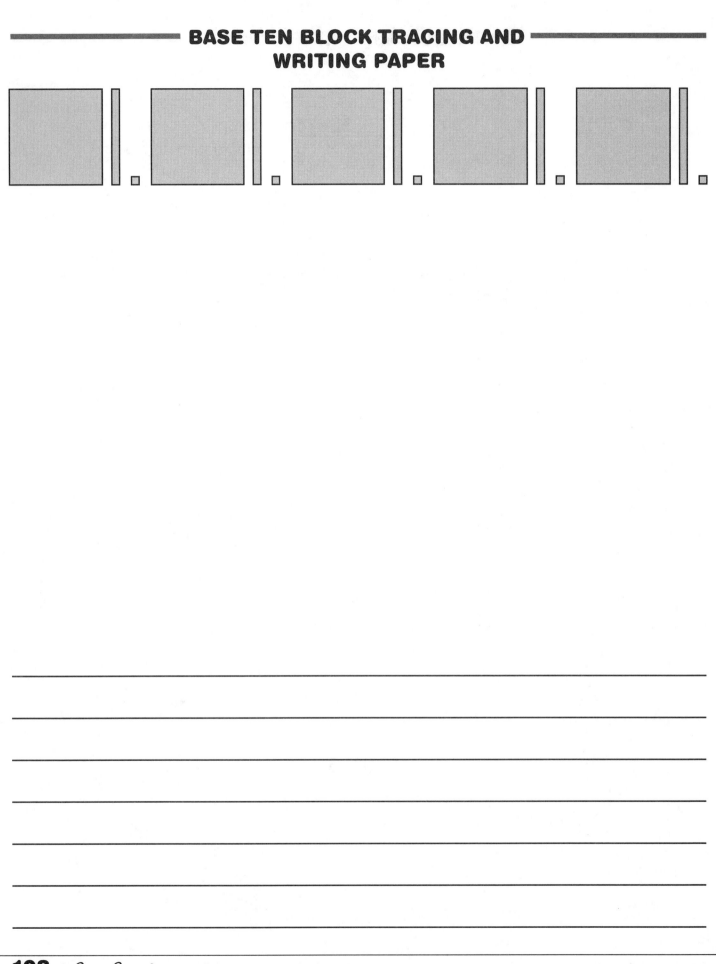

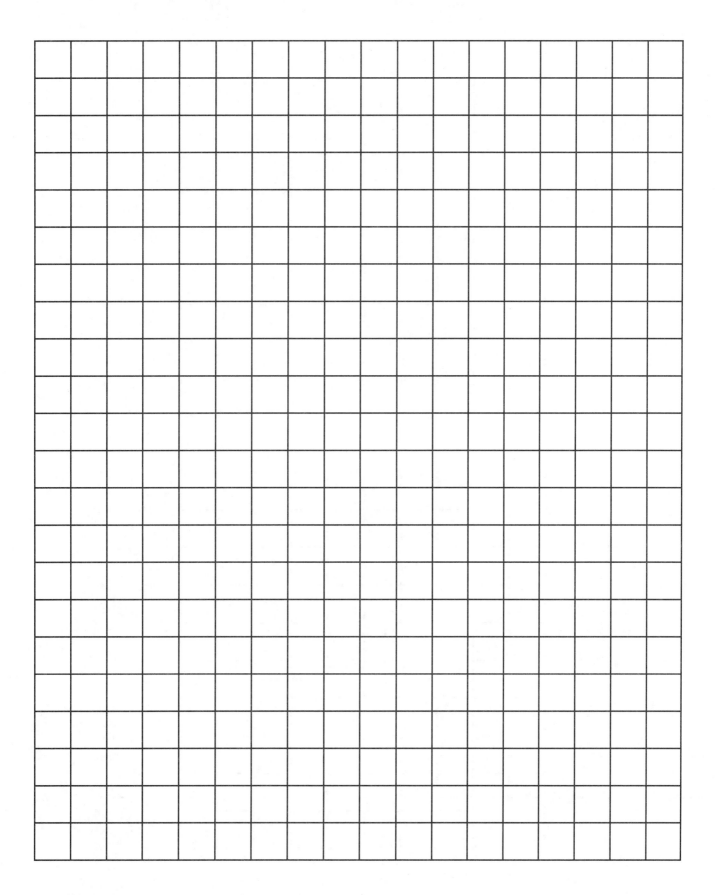

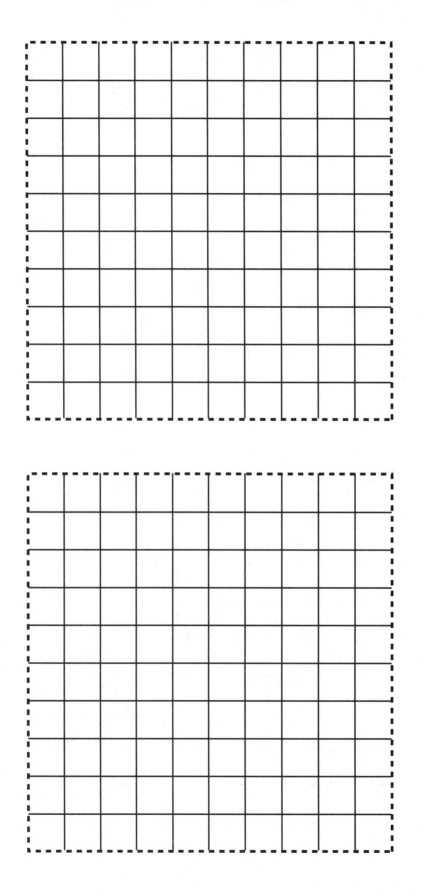